The Therapy Manifesto:
95 Treatises on Holodynamic Therapy

Books by Victor Vernon Woolf, Ph.D.

Holodynamics: How to Develop and Manage Your Personal Power
The original 1990 text outlining the basic principles of Holodynamics.

The Dance of Life: Transform your life NOW! Create wellness, resolve conflict and harmonize your "Being" with Nature.
Published in 2005, this text exemplifies the multiple dimensions of consciousness within reality and shows how this information applies in solving complex problems of the World.

Five Manuals that Accompany "The Dance of Life"
Sequential Manuals, published in 2005 and 2006, that provide both an expansion of the theoretical premises and specific training exercises for those who want to apply Holodynamics and include the following:

Manual 1. The Holodynamic State of Being
Advocates a course in life that unfolds one's fullest potential for the individual and for the planet.

Manual 2. Presence in a Conscious Universe
Detailed training in achieving the state of being present, aligning with one's Full Potential Self, bonding with others, Tracking and transforming holodynes and unfolding of potential.

Manual 3. Field Shifting: The Holodynamics of Integration
Training exercises for integration of field of information from the past, present and future through the "Re-live/Pre-live" processes.

Manual 4. Leadership and Teambuilding: The Holodynamics of Building a New World
The use of a holodynamic approach within systems, such as in business and education.

Manual 5. Principle-Driven Transformation: The Holodynamics of the Dance of Life
The principles, processes, and stories that form the basis for teaching Holodynamics.

The Wellness Manifesto: 95 Treatises on Holodynamic Health
An outline of 95 findings from current sciences that apply to the theory and practice of healing.

Elves: The Adventures Of Nicholas: The Grid Of Agony And The Field Of Love
A science-fiction story about time-traveling Elves who live according to the principles and processes of holodynamic consciousness and become involved in an intergalactic battle that sweeps a small boy, Nicholas Claus, into helping shift the grid of agony into a field of love. How Christmas began.

Intimacy: Develop your Being of Togetherness: How to Create an Open, Dynamic, Effective, Intimate, Living Relationship with Someone You Love

The above writings can be purchased at www.holodynamics.com/store.asp

THE THERAPY MANIFESTO

THE THERAPY MANIFESTO:

95 TREATISES ON HOLODYNAMIC THERAPY

By
Victor Vernon Woolf, Ph.D., A.A.M.F.T.

The Therapy Manifesto:
95 Treatises on Holodynamic Therapy

Original Illustrations by the author
Cover by Charles Montague
Editing by Catherine Rourke
Graphic design by Debbie Drecksel
Others by permission as noted

Library of Congress Cataloging-in-Publication Data

Woolf, Victor Vernon
The Therapy Manifesto: 95 Treatises on Holodynamic Therapy

ISBN 0-9746431-6-5
1. Therapy. 2. Psychology. 3. Science. 4. Consciousness.
5. Cosmology. 6. Self-Organizing Information Systems.
7. Quantum Theory. 8. Self Help. 9. Title

PRINTED IN THE UNITED STATES OF AMERICA

Publisher: The International Academy of Holodynamics
1155 West 4th Street, Suite 214, Reno, NV 89503

Additional copies of this text may be obtained directly through www.holodynamics.com
or from your local distributor.

TABLE OF CONTENTS

Preface   x

Introduction   xi
   New discoveries of science that apply to therapy..xiv
   My personal experience as a therapist xv
   The Holodynamics of therapy xvi

CHAPTER ONE: THE SCIENCE OF THERAPY   2
   1. Therapy is holodynamic...3
   2. Therapy is multidimensional 3
   3. The universe is conscious...3
   4. Consciousness is hyperspacial..4
   5. Reality is holographic 4
   6. Holodynes and the power to cause 4
   7. Consciousness is quantum...5

CHAPTER TWO: THE MULTIPLE DIMENSIONS OF THERAPY   10
   8. The Full Potential Self – our "counterpart in hyperspace" 11
   9. Multiple definitions of "self" 11
  10. The "primary reference" for individual therapy is personal potential 12
  11. "I" am always bigger than "my problem"...12
  12. Relationship therapy references the "Being Of Togetherness"...............12

CHAPTER THREE: THERAPY AS THE TRANSFORMATION OF INFORMA-
TION   18
  13. Transformation of information 19
  14. Therapy identifies, explores and transforms holodynes.........................19
  15. Therapy follows the implicate order 20

CHAPTER FOUR: THERAPY IS SELF-INITIATED   24
  16. Therapy promotes self-initiated change 25
  17. Therapy creates a menu of options..25
  18. Therapy facilitates choice 25
  19. Therapy is self-organizing...26
  20. Therapy is self-realizing 26
  21. Therapy is committed to self-initiated action 26

CHAPTER FIVE: THERAPY PROCESSES   32
  22. Therapy advocates equality..33
  23. Therapy is not bound by time..33
  24. Therapeutic dimensions rise beyond linear or physical models.............34

25. Therapy helps create a state of being at peace.. 34
26. Therapy accesses the holographic dimension of holodynes........................... 34
27. The transformation of emotions through "Tracking" 35
28. Shifting collective consciousness through the "Re-live/Pre-live" processes 35
29. Potentialization.. 36
30. Our "bond" with the past and future 36

CHAPTER SIX: BIOLOGICAL ASPECTS OF THERAPY　　　　**42**
31. The dimensions of hyperspace and our DNA... 43
32. Unlimited energy.. 43
33. Unfolding personal and collective potential 44

CHAPTER SEVEN: THERAPEUTIC SOLUTIONS　　　　**50**
34. Problems are caused by their solutions... 51
35. Solutions within enfolded information systems 51
36. Solutions within symbiotic life forms 52
37. Solutions from inherited holodynes 52
38. Solutions from internal coherence processes 53
39. Solutions from parallel worlds 53
40. Solutions from our collective covenant.. 53
41. Solutions and the environment for change 54
42. Solutions beyond the emotional model.. 54
43. Solutions beyond the rational model 55
44. Solutions from transformation of the past.. 55
45. Solutions from the future 55
46. Solutions as integration 56

CHAPTER EIGHT: THERAPY AND THE OPEN MARKET　　　　**64**
47. Therapy as a "product" on the open market 65
48. Therapy is effective and efficient.. 65

CHAPTER NINE: WHO IS THE THERAPIST?　　　　**68**
49. Therapists are "present" 69
50. The therapist is transparent.. 69
51. The therapist is both "in" and "out" of the therapy process 69
52. The therapist is accountable... 70
53. The therapists and participants are part of the same field......................... 70
54. The therapist "is" the therapy 70

CHAPTER TEN: THERAPY AND TECHNOLOGY　　　　**74**
55. Therapy tools include the Internet.. 75
56. There are no hidden agendas in therapy... 75
57. People-to-people versus doctor-to-patient 75

CHAPTER ELEVEN: THERAPY AND THE "COMPANY" 80

58. Pharmaceutical companies and professional therapists are also people too 81
59. The company cannot prescribe therapy 81
60. Company diagnostic tools don't work 81
61. Presence subverts hierarchies 82
62. Therapy cannot depend upon drugs 82
63. People are insulated against advertising 82
64. Therapy cannot be conducted from an ivory tower 83
65. There are no secrets 83

CHAPTER TWELVE: WHAT IS THERAPY? 88

66. Therapy is a covenant 89
67. Therapy is a dynamic exchange of information 89
68. Therapy is a conscious experience 90
69. Therapy is a multidimensional conversation 90
70. Therapy is an alignment 90
71. Therapy is collaborative 91
72. Therapy is a family affair - a living, intimate Being of Togetherness 91
73. Therapy is a community activity 91
74. Therapy is life-enhancing 91
75. Therapy is a balancing act 92
76. Therapy ends when more than one conversation is taking place 92
77. Therapy explores beyond the firewalls of command and control ...92
78. Therapy is integration 93
79. Therapy is the "emerging" of a new state of being 93
80. Therapy is a process 94
81. The old therapy doesn't work anymore 94
82. The therapist talks with people at their own level 94
83. People know things too 95
84. Therapy is co-authorship 95
85. Therapy reflects our symbiotic relationship to reality 95
86. Therapy is unique 96
87. Therapy maintains a superposition 96

CHAPTER THIRTEEN: THE RESULTS OF THERAPY 102

88. Psychological well-being 103
89. Integrated swarm intelligence 103
90. Coherence 104
91. Personal superposition 104

CHAPTER FOURTEEN: THERAPY AS A PUBLIC TRUST 108

92. What the future holds for therapy 109
93. Therapists realize that their potential markets are laughing at them 109
94. Therapy is an open door 110
95. Therapy is a public trust 110

GLOSSARY OF TERMS   115
ACKNOWLEDGEMENTS   126
REFERENCES   127
AFTERWORD   132

Note: The reference numbers *1 through 95* used in the text refer to the footnote sections at the end of each chapter. The footnotes are numbered according to each treatise so the reader can better identify the source of the facts presented, and more details are discussed. Writings mentioned in the text can be found in the reference section at the end of the text.

PREFACE

This Manifesto is necessary because new discoveries of science have revealed information that has a profound effect on both the theory and the practice of therapy. This new information has its origins in sciences known as quantum physics, holographics, information theory, superconductivity, biophysics, chaos theory and others that are now reflected in the science of consciousness. Every therapist will want to become familiar with this new information because it reflects remarkable development in the field of consciousness.

Almost every tenant of therapy is challenged by these new findings. They demonstrate that everything is made of holographic information "spinners" that are multidimensional and hyperspacial. Everything physical has a counterpart in hyperspace. From this perspective, consciousness is not confined to the human brain or neural system but manifests throughout the body and even throughout society. Our thoughts are quantum. Furthermore, consciousness is shared with the universe. Everything and everyone is quantum in nature. Everything is driven by potential and, in some context, interconnected.

The application of this information has been thoroughly tested and applied to thousands of cases within both the therapy clinic setting and among the general public through education and self-help programs in different cultures. This approach has created extraordinary therapeutic movement and, in many parts of the world, it has become known as "Holodynamic Psychology." This Manifesto is written, in part, to clarify the distinctions made in what has become known as "the Holodynamic approach" to therapy.

The scientific basis of this Manifesto is contained in the 95 treatises that are considered central to both the theory and practice of therapy. Each treatise is based upon information from associated sciences that has been successfully assimilated into the practice of therapy and tested multiculturally. Each has been found to create positive results in therapeutic movement. A footnote section is provided that outlines supportive research and other related scientific data. A reference section is also provided, along with a bibliography of terms, and a reference section.

INTRODUCTION

Centuries ago "therapy" came from the root word *theros* meaning "from God," or literally, "a return to God." This translation has evolved until it has come to mean "a reunion to wholeness," or "mental health." Living as we do, in an industrialized society, therapy has been in such demand that the search for mental health has become a multi-billion dollar industry. In response to the public demand, several disciplines are currently responsible for mental health. These include: psychiatry, psychology, social work, marriage and family therapy, as well as other public agencies, including educational and court associated counseling.

In addition, more than a dozen schools of thought have emerged that deal with the theoretical frameworks woven into the practice of therapy. In *The Dance of Life* (2005), these primary schools of thought are discussed in more detail. Briefly, they include: cognitive science, quantum consciousness, neuropsychology, clinical psychology, individual psychotherapy, self-referencing, developmental psychology, social psychology, spiritualism, altered states of being, subtle energies and Holodynamics.[1] This information is not repeated in this writing but is recommended for those who are interested in the broader context of consciousness.

What makes the practice of therapy more complex is the fact that new findings of various branches of science have discovered a great deal of information about the nature of reality and, particularly, about the nature of human consciousness. Many of these findings were not known until recently. As a result, in the last few years, more information has been gathered about the nature of reality and about human consciousness than in the entire prior history of humankind. Therapists need to put this new information to work in their therapy practice, and this text is an attempt to meet this need.

Along with this new body of information, there are new technologies and lifestyle developments that have changed the way people live. This includes the way they think and feel. In some parts of the world, these new developments have flooded the market and changed the way people relate to one another, how families deal with each other, and how people do business. Along with this flood of new technology and dynamic changes in society, we are now experiencing a literal explosion of information about human consciousness. The entire picture of mental health and mental illness is undergoing a remarkable transformation. We know more about overcoming mental illness now than ever before and most therapists are not yet aware of this transformation. We have entered a new age – the Age of Consciousness - and therapists are expected to be aware of these developments, how they came about, and how to apply them in their therapy practice.

Take, for example, the developments within science. Most people are aware that a great battle has been raging among intellectuals regarding the nature of reality. This battle has been mostly between those who viewed reality in a *mechanistic* view (as in classical or particle physics) and those who viewed reality as *wave dynamics* (as in quantum physics). Most therapy models were designed from a classical view of reality. Some are now adopting a more quantum view, but few people realize that human consciousness operates beyond the confines of either of these branches of science.

It is now recognized that classical physics is able to describe reality within a limited range (approximately 10 to the plus and minus 7) while quantum physics is able to expand this range (10 to the plus and minus 14). Yet human consciousness functions at an even broader range (10 to the minus 33 for Frohlech frequencies within the microtubules, for example). This expanded range of reality requires a new approach – one that encompasses the whole dynamic of consciousness and the whole dynamic of reality.

Even though quantum sciences have doubled the scope and predictability of physics and even though almost half of all recent inventions are based upon their findings, it takes an even more expanded view of reality to understand the mechanisms and the processes of consciousness. Consciousness operates within the ranges of both classical and quantum dynamics but many things, including consciousness, operate from beyond these ranges. In order to facilitate mental health, a therapist must understand the findings of both of these branches of science and then move beyond the range of both into the dimensions of hyperspace and subtle forces. The therapist must become aware of the whole dynamic. In other words, therapists must become holodynamic.

I like Paul Townsend's approach as a theoretical physicist because his model identifies at least 10 dimensions of reality that are enfolded within what we experience with our senses and what exists in reality. Our normal senses only pick up four dimensions (width, depth, breadth and time) and yet, according to Townsend, there are enfolded dimensions that are just as real and just as important as the ones we can sense. Furthermore, he declares, "All dimensions are created equal." [2]

In order to be therapeutic, we must become aware of any dimensions that are involved with consciousness. Since everything is made of information in motion, everything is, in some dimension, conscious. Therapist must then become aware of the whole dynamic. The whole dynamic means that all branches of science, whether classical or quantum, can be included in the therapeutic framework. Furthermore, all dimensions of reality must also be included in the framework of the therapist. We must have any information that is applicable to both the theory and practice of therapy. Holographics, information theory, photonics, Genomics, evolutionary anthropology and many "alternative" approaches to healing are painting a new picture about mental health.

In order to be an effective therapist, one must understand not only the battles going on among the scientists, but also therapy practices of the past have been dominated by assumptions proven to be anything but therapeutic. Some of these assumptions arise from the way information self-organizes. Thus many of our embedded beliefs, taboos, rituals and social patterns that arose from religious, spiritualism and mythological procedures and assumptions of the past often had little to do with reality.

Over the last few centuries, these assumptions have been challenged first by classical physics and lately by quantum physics. Now the new information from science has penetrated into society's biological, physiological, psychological and social counterparts. It's turning out to be a whole new ball game and part of that game is to integrate the new information into a working therapeutic model, test the model and, if it works, let others know about it.

While this integration has been helpful, it is clear that the limitations of the classical sciences have kept the entire field of therapy locked into highly restrictive mechanistic models that often proved to be counter-therapeutic. As therapists, we have all been trained under this restrictive framework. As a result, we have been losing ground, so to speak, as far as helping the public "return to wholeness and mental health." It is evident that people have not yet become mentally and emotionally healthy. Those who have picked up the assumptions of quantum physics have adapted their approaches to "energy" and "wave" dynamics and, this, too, has led to approaches that are anything but therapeutic.

This does not mean that our scientific approach hasn't helped. Both the classical and the quantum view have broadened our perspectives. What is happening in our collective consciousness is that innovative information from new and different branches of science has shed considerable light on mental illnesses. Information is expanding beyond the confines of the mechanistic and quantum frameworks and into the science of consciousness. New facts are now available about consciousness. Not only are these facts now public knowledge but they can easily be seen when one compares the major schools of thought regarding therapy to the known mechanisms of consciousness. [1]

What becomes clear is that, in both the theory and the practice of therapy, the entire schools of psychiatry, psychology, sociology, family therapy and related practices have generally fallen *behind the times*.[1] It is evident from both the theory and practice of therapy that therapists understand less than half of the basic essential *mechanisms* of consciousness, let alone the more than a dozen *dimensions* of consciousness. They have failed to apply the new scientific information to therapy. Collectively, we have failed to keep the public trust. This is the main reason for this Manifesto. Therapists need to catch up on what is known.

Absorbing new information from various fields of science is a difficult task for those who have an active client load. Not only do we lack the time to study different disciplines, but the new information requires changing our thinking - not just about therapy, but about the nature of reality. The new discoveries challenge both our traditional views and our practices of therapy. In spite of everything we have been taught in the old, now outdated schools from which we obtained our licensure, this new information cannot be avoided. What emerges from the new sciences is a view of the universe as a conscious, interconnected, multidimensional, dynamic information system. We are holodynamic.[1]

This new information is flooding into the public domain. Those entering into the therapy process will understand this new information and will seek to apply it in their lives and use it in their therapy processes. As therapists we have an obligation to be informed on all aspects of human consciousness. The practice of therapy is a public trust. Governments and private groups have established schools, licensure and funding in order to ensure that this public trust is maintained and therapists have become the holders of that trust.

As we attempt to come to grips with the new information, we must address the impact the new discoveries have on our understanding of human nature and the practical applications the information has in the day-to-day practice of therapy. In order to make this possible, I have outlined in brief a few examples that are discussed in more detail in the 95 treatises that compose the body of this text.

New discoveries in Science that apply to therapy:

Some of these new discoveries include the following:

a. *Multiple, enfolded mechanisms of consciousness*
b. *The central role of microtubules in consciousness*
c. *Multidimensional dynamics within the microtubules*
d. *Holographic memory storage units (holodynes) that control both body and behavior*
e. *Quantum dynamics in neurological systems, creation of coherence, telepathic tunneling and collective fields of potential*
f. *Hyperspacial networks of information spinners, precomputations and our hyperspacial counterpart (Full Potential Self)*
g. *How holodynes are created, inherited, modeled by family and culture and come from hyperspacial dimensions*
h. *How collective consciousness, or swarm intelligence, operates to affect and often control psychological well-being*
i. *The fine-grained and gross-grained screens that cover the senses of the human body and create the holographic matrix controlling perception and information processing, memory recall and human behavior*
j. *Frequencies used to both send and receive information, thus creating quantum coherence in the body and affecting multiple dimensions of consciousness*
k. *Effective principles and processes for creating psychological health, etc.*

To date there are at least 20 known natural mechanisms of consciousness that directly relate to therapy. Most therapy approaches, both in theory and in practice, have not yet included many of these aspects of consciousness in their approach to therapy.[1] To the degree that they are not included, therapy can fall short of its intended goal of the return of psychological well-being.

One dimension, for example, is the hyperspacial dimension. Therapy can provide the opportunity for people to access their hyperspacial counterpart, their Full Potential Self. Both in theory and practice, one can align with one's hyperspacial counterpart and unfold the fullest individual potential possible. Hyperspace is a known dimension in science and, when this information is applied to therapy, it produces extraordinary therapeutic movement.

Another dimension of consciousness is provided by the science of holographics. When a therapist adopts a holographic context, information is viewed as holographic in form. From this framework, it is possible to access the holographic dimension of consciousness where "holodynes" are found. Holodynes are self-organizing information systems (formed within the microtubules) and basically in charge of all thinking and feeling processes. Therapy is an opportunity to transform holodynes and thus improve quality of life. The subconscious becomes conscious. The patient is able to access, understand and transform those information systems that were once considered so problematic. This transformation process follows a built-in order of development.

These treatises bring each of the enfolded dimensions of reality directly into the theory and practice of therapy. Each dimension of reality is interactive with the consciousness of each person. As each dimension is more clearly understood, the interconnection among the entire field of consciousness becomes evident. Therapy becomes holodynamic. Both the therapist and those who participate in therapy understand how their holodynes control their holographic screens that control their perception of reality. They grasp how, by transforming holodynes, they can change their experience of reality both internally and collectively. Furthermore, it is possible to shift the field of consciousness hyperspacially and integrate the parallel worlds of the past and future with the present.

Such activities cannot be fathomed from a traditionalistic, linear mentality. The new sciences have thrust open the doors of past restrictions, and therapists are entrusted to close the time lapse between these recent discoveries of science and their applications in the practice of therapy.

My Personal Experiences as a Therapist

I became aware of these implications more than 30 years ago and began to research how these new principles of science could apply to the theory and practice of therapy. My background in physics, education, world religions and developmental psychology provided a comfortable basis for me. I loved the new sciences. I became an avid reader and absorbed everything I could get my hands on. Once I realized that everything was made of information in motion and this information was all interconnected, I could embrace the idea that reality was one interconnected unified field.

Each science brought new details as to the nature of reality. Everything was driven by potential. Everything was made of information in motion. Everything was conscious. We are part of a multidimensional, conscious universe. We are holodynamic. The applications of a holodynamic view resulted in extraordinary therapeutic movement for my clients. My private therapy sessions focused on the holographic information systems that control human behavior and how such systems could be transformed. This framework generated remarkable life changes for my clients, and my therapy processes quickly evolved into short-term, self-directed procedures.

Applying these principles within the drug abuse population in six cities resulted in a society that became essentially free of illegal drug pushing. When we taught these principles and processes to families of patients in the State Mental Hospital in Utah, these efforts resulted in more than 81% drop in the patient load of the hospital. Similar results have been achieved with prison populations, among juvenile offenders and street gangs in Los Angeles, California.

These principles were also applied in business and churches, and perhaps the most dynamic applications to date have come from the political and military arenas. We used them in helping to bring an end to the Cold War and in efforts to transform war mentalities in the Middle East. In general, the application of this information produces extraordinary therapeutic results no matter how complex the problems seem to appear. We discovered that every problem is both created and driven by its potential solution.

The Holodynamics of Therapy:

Understanding the holodynamic nature of our conscious universe gives people a view far beyond the linear, diagnostic or mechanistic models of most past therapies. In order for modern therapy to reach its fullest potential and meet the demands of an educated and informed public, therapy must get out of the office and into the streets where people live. Therapy is needed in the home, the workplace and in the political arena. Therapists must become more holodynamic because neither the individual nor the therapy process can be isolated from the whole dynamic. One must ask how, for example, therapeutic input could potentially influence the "war mentality" that is so prevalent in our society today and how public response could be influenced toward transformation of "cause" rather than striking out against apparent symptoms.

"Cause" includes the Holodynamics of hyperspacial information fields of parallel worlds, including the person's counterpart or Full Potential Self, along with information from the past and future. Potentially, the therapist might be able to transform the collective into a field of wellness and environmental balance as well as any other fields where a return to health might be activated. The new information indicates that every problem is caused by its solution. Solutions are sometimes multidimensional. Therapy must be multidimensional.

It is possible to grasp the multidimensional aspects of therapy by viewing reality from within an expanded framework. Most people understand that they were born within a family that is part of a community. We recognize that our community is part of a larger city that is part of a larger state that is part of a nation that is part of the world. The therapist recognizes that each person has a certain amount of self-interest that must be negotiated in order for the individual to have his or her needs met. The same is true of each collective entity in the matrix in which we all find ourselves embedded.

The therapy framework must include the ability to facilitate negotiated self-interest at all levels of reality, including family, social, national and global levels. In this sense, therapy has a vital role to play in dealing with personal, family and cultural beliefs. In a world that uses religion as a part of war, our collective beliefs require a therapeutic touch that reaches beyond the individual into the field of our collective consciousness, including business, culture, religion, military and government. Therapy has a professional, moral and ethical responsibility to deal with the whole dynamic of consciousness. Therapists must reach, not only into the depths of personal consciousness, but also into the depth and breath of collective consciousness.

As therapists we are also challenged to understand the multiple dimensions of consciousness, including the physics and biology of consciousness, the impact of our inner body life forms, genetic inheritance of information and the quantum dynamics of consciousness. Such factors have direct impact upon consciousness. There is no doubt these enfolded dimensions are causing mental illness. If therapists expect to function in any sense as stewards of a healthier state of consciousness for individuals, they must also be able to respond to the causal field dynamics of families and society and must be aware of the whole dynamic of consciousness. They must be "therapeutic" to the benefit of all because, according to physics, everything is connected.

For many therapists, this challenge may seem "unattainable. I am here to testify that it is not only attainable, but that it is not that difficult. The information required is already within our field of consciousness. All that is required is learning to access the information and apply it in a therapeutic way.

One of the marvels of our modern age is the world's recent explosion in the development of technology. Any person, at the touch of their fingertips on the Internet, can access the most current information about consciousness and its possible applications to therapy. We all live in an amazing era in which, as therapists, we have the opportunity to utilize the revolutionary changes in telecommunications and help the public throw off the blanket of secrecy that previously covered therapy practices. Therapy is rapidly losing its mystery, and people are able to glean immense amounts of information on how to heal their emotional and mental disorders.

New information leads to new expectations and new awareness. This phenomenon of "newness" has created a new kind of participant – one with the ability to evaluate his or her problem prior to applying for therapy and one with ability to evaluate the therapist as well. Participants are demanding new approaches to therapy since former "patients" are now becoming "co-participants" who are sometimes better educated than the therapist and, in addition, are more personally responsible for all aspects of their own mental health.

Add to that, a mobile world where people are traveling much of the time and cannot afford the past luxury of an office visit. They want and often demand immediate, sustained, long-distance therapeutic consultation. In a society where change is the norm, therapy is needed as never before in history to add the threads of integration and meaning in an ever-changing world. Therapists are facing new circumstances. There are new rules. There is new information. Therapists must adapt so their service can survive and thrive.

The 95 Treatises on Holodynamic Therapy that follow outline some of the new challenges from science and technology that applies to therapy. It is self-evident that the following treatise is not the final word but only an introduction to an ongoing collaboration among all those interested in furthering the therapy process of producing psychological health and well-being.

CHAPTER ONE

THE SCIENCE OF THERAPY

*T*HE SCIENCE OF THERAPY

1. Therapy is Holodynamic

In physics, there is a web of relationships called dualities,[1] which indicate everything is made of dynamic information fields that are connected to one another. In other words, the world is one, whole dynamic information system or "holodynamic."[1,2] Because of its public trust, therapy is concerned with any significant information within the whole dynamic of reality, so therapy is holodynamic.

2. Therapy is multidimensional

It is a generally accepted scientific framework that there are at least *10 dimensions* enfolded into physical reality.[2] Traditionally, at least up until the last few decades, science and therapy have been based upon a four-dimensional model of reality wherein we experience depth, width, height and the passage of time. With the unveiling of multiple dimensions of reality comes new understanding of the multidimensional nature of consciousness and thus a multidimensional approach to therapy.

In a world made up of hyperspacial information spinners, quantum potential fields, holographic dynamics, quantum forces, Frohlech frequencies and parallel worlds, therapy must deal with these various enfolded dimensions because they are known to influence human consciousness.[1] The public trust requires that therapists understand these enfolded dimensions of consciousness and how they influence personal reality and the therapeutic process.

3. The Universe is conscious

Everything, all matter and all life forms, is made of information networks that are both dynamic and enfolded within multiple dimensions.[3] What this means is that *everything is made of dynamic information networks* that are *intimately interwoven into the fabric of space and time.* Everything is conscious and consciousness is multidimensional.

Being a therapist requires that we understand the dynamics of these networks of consciousness. Thus, consciousness itself is a quality of reality, intimately interconnected within the fabric of space and time. [1,2] Being a therapist requires that we understand the dynamic and universal nature of consciousness and apply this to the therapy experience. Any aspect of consciousness could potentially contain information that could either block or benefit therapeutic movement.

4. Consciousness is hyperspacial

Another enfolded dimension of reality is its hyperspacial (faster than the speed of light) connection.[4] Matter, that is, every subatomic particle, every atom, molecule and every living system, has a hyperspacial counterpart that gives *form* to our physical world. Our physical world and our hyperspacial dimension have a one-to-one relationship and cannot be separated. These dimensions are connected to all other dimensions. Information continually exchanges between hyperspace and the physical world. This information is manifest in multiple dimensions, including multiple histories from the past and future. [1,2]

It was Roger Penrose, the neurological expert who is also one of the world's great mathematicians and a quantum physicist, who pointed out that, before we think a thought, our counterpart in some hyperspacial, parallel dimension, has already pre-computed our menu of choices regarding that thought. These hyperspacial dimensions bring into the therapy experience the possibility of powerful influences from hyperspacial parallel dimensions and how these influences can be used in the therapy process.

5. Reality is holographic

A hologram is a three dimensional image imprinted upon a two dimensional page. The holographic principle demonstrates that a complex information system, with multiple dimensions, can project itself upon a less complex, fewer-dimensioned reality.[5]

When scientists apply the holographic principle to black holes, two more dimensions of reality become evident, making it possible to understand the flow of information into and out of black holes. Without this holographic understanding, we would not be able to explain either black holes or many other aspects of reality.

Likewise, human consciousness, with its complex dimensions, can be explained more fully when the holographic principle is applied. The holographic nature of consciousness is essential in the therapy process because all thought forms, including our mental and emotional patterns, are holographic. [1]

6. Holodynes and the power to cause

The application of the holographic principle to the dimensions of consciousness reveals the enfolded dimension of *holodynes*.[1,6] Holodynes are holographic images stored within the water media of our microtubules.

These multidimensional information systems turn out to be self-organizing and self-perpetuating, and they have developed the power to cause. Holodynes are, in fact, involved in all human behavior because human behavior is caused by information stored within the micro-tubules. This information is stored holographically as holodynes.

Holodynes are also quantum in nature. They also experience growth. They have stages of development, can communicate and be transformed. Dealing with the dimension of holo-dynes has proven central to effective therapy processes.

7. Consciousness is quantum

Another enfolded dimension of consciousness is its quantum nature.[7] Consciousness is interwoven with quantum frequencies, harmonics, potential fields and states of being.

Quantum physics is recognized as the most accurate and comprehensive science yet de-vised. It is responsible for more than 40 percent of all new inventions of the past few decades, made possible the harnessing of atomic power and helping us reach the moon.

One of the discoveries of quantum physicists is that consciousness is quantum. It is non-linear, hyperspacial and collective in nature. These facts have profound implications for therapy.

From a quantum view, life emerges from a quantum potential field and influences vari-ous holodynes via quantum frequencies. Life can be viewed as a natural process of unfolding potential. Life potential is enfolded within the quantum potential field. Since therapy is about living a healthy life, therapy is about the quantum dynamics of unfolding potential. Quantum life potential holds an essential key to personal and collective mental health.

FOOTNOTES - CHAPTER ONE

1. Reality (and thus Therapy) is Holodynamic: In physics, this is referred to as "M-theory" wherein the five current string theories and at least 10 dimensions of reality are considered different expressions of one underlying reality. There are many books and articles written on the holodynamic nature of the universe. See *Holodynamics: How to Manage Your Personal Power*, 1990; and *The Dance of Life: Transform your world NOW!* 2005 by Victor Vernon Woolf; *The Holographic Universe*, Mike Talbot; or Ken Wilber's *The Holographic Paradigm*. For a brief summary of "M-theory" and holographics, see *The Universe in a Nutshell*, Stephen Hawking, 2001.

2. Reality (and thus therapy) is multidimensional: The multidimensional nature of the universe is an accepted scientific framework. Paul Townsend, of Cambridge University for example, has devised a model of at least a 10-dimensional universe in order to explain such things as the forces of gravity. Each dimension is seen as "enfolded" within the others. He refers to these dimensions as "P-branes," where "P" stands for the number of one through 10, etc., and "branes" represents the "dimensions" included in one's framework. See *The Universe in a Nutshell*, by Stephen Hawking for more details. See also Footnotes 4 and 6 below.

3. Consciousness (and thus therapy) is universal: The premises for this statement were laid in 1984 in private conversations with David Bohm, who is recognized as one of the founding fathers of quantum physics. (See *Wholeness and the Implicate Order*). At that conference, 34 of the world's leading thinkers in quantum physics gathered at Temple University. After almost two days of intense discussion on various aspects of reality, I asked David Bohm, "What known influence could possibly have initiated the collapse of the quantum field?" I never forgot his answer: "The only cause that we can identify in the universe that creates the collapse of the wave is intelligence itself."

It was Bohm's position that everything was connected to a quantum potential field made of information. From this point, consciousness may impact reality. I surmised later that perhaps consciousness, or at least its influence, is the secret force in Einstein's "cosmic constant." All speculation aside, there is now ample evidence to demonstrate that even photons are "conscious." See Kevin Kelly, *Out of Control*, Bohm, *Wholeness and the Implicate Order*. See also Woolf, *The Dance of Life: Transform your world NOW!* or *The Universe in a Nutshell*, by Stephen Hawking 2001.

4. Consciousness (and thus therapy) is hyperspacial: The works of Roger Penrose and Stewart Hameroff have impacted the scientific world over the past decade with their "(OR) Orch" model of consciousness. Their research suggests that "hyperspacial, quantum networks of entangled spinner information system" are "pre-computing options" before we are actually conscious of what is going on. Consciousness is "pre-computed" in this "hyperspacial" or "faster than the speed of light" dimension, giving it expression in this space-time continuum.

This information has been the focus of conferences around the world for the past few years. (Refer to the "Science of Consciousness" conferences held each year in Tucson, Arizona, and sponsored by the University of Arizona). Our entire history of humankind is replete with examples of paranormal phenomenon and influences suggesting dimensions faster than physical temporal existence. (See reference section with regard to Penrose, Hameroff, Hawking and Woolf for further study).

5. The holographic nature of consciousness: The applications of the holographic view on the nature of consciousness have impacted both the theory and practice of therapy. Findings of multidimensional physics, in which "higher-dimensions" are "curled up within our four-dimensional space-time," demonstrate how people think. Stephen Hawking, for example, suggest we "live in a four-dimensional world because we are shadows cast on the brane (this dimension) by what is happening in the interior of the bubble." According to this view, our universe is a holographic projection emanating from more complex dimensions of hyperspace. Everything in the universe is conscious, caused by a series of connections with hyperspace in superposition. See Stephen Hawking, *The Universe in a Nutshell*, 2001 Pp. 197-199. See also references outlined in 1-4 above and 6 below.

6. Multidimensional, holographic memory storage units - "holodynes" and how they function to control both body and behavior: This view was originally based upon the mathematical proofs found in Brown's book, *Laws of Form*. This work is now widely correlated with information theory and the science of consciousness. Paul Townsend's model of *p-branes*, from applied mathematics and theoretical physics, is one example.

In Townsend's model, a "p-brane" has length in p direction. When p = 1, only one dimension of reality is considered. So, in a *1-brane* model of existence, reality appears as a string (as in breadth). In a *2-brane* world, reality is a surface (as in breadth and width). In a *3-brane* world, reality appears in three dimensions (as in width, breadth and height) and reality is a cube. A surface with three dimensions experiencing the passage of time would be a *p = 4* or *4-brane* world, as in our space-time world. In order to explain the nature of gravity, for example, Townsend demonstrates a model that requires *p=10* or *p=11* dimensions.

Since we all recognize the forces of gravity, our world has a greater number of dimensions than what appears to our ordinary senses. Following Bohm's model, these dimensions would be "enfolded" and make up the "implicate order" of reality.

From the findings of developmental psychology, it is evident that consciousness has enfolded, within it, multiple dimensions of reality. Depending upon the number of these dimensions used by researchers, various stages of development of consciousness can be seen to emerge.

Early researchers, such as Piaget and Kohlberg, for example, attempted to identify various stages of development of young people, and then adults. These early findings have been correlated to various schools of thought in psychology, education, religion and other social systems (see Woolf 1990, 2005). Recent research into memory storage and mechanisms of consciousness, and their corresponding dimensions of reality, carry consciousness into hyperspacial dimensions where their ancient interpretation of the past can be correlated with the present and the future. These processes allow therapeutic integration but, in order to undertake these processes, it is necessary to access enfolded dimensions.

One of these dimensions is holographics. It is evident from history and science that this is a holographic universe. So memory storage and human behavior is holographic in nature (see Woolf, 1990, 2005,2006 and items 1-6 above).

Holographics refers to images produced from the interaction of a reference wave and an information wave as they interact on a photographic plate. By shining a light through the plate, a three-dimensional image is produced. This is called a hologram. When the plate is broken and a light is shone through a single piece of the plate, the entire image can still be produced. [2]

Research by Karl Pribram, et al, shows that fine-grained and gross-grained screens that create the holographic effect in perception and memory storage cover the senses. It is evident that our sensory mechanisms and our memory storage processes are holographic. Thus the nature of memory and of consciousness not only includes holographic mechanisms, but it also includes Holodynamics. Consciousness is holodynamic.

7. Therapy is quantum: Nearly a century has elapsed since Niels Bohr suggested that the atomic structure of atoms was a "harmonic" of "information in motion" (also referred to as "standing waves"). This is considered by most scientists as a giant step forward from the classical view of atoms as a series of solid little "billiard balls" rotating around each other. The result was the birth of quantum mechanics and quantum physics. The classical Newtonian view of physics, or "particle" science, had ruled the thinking of almost every school of thought until the dawn of quantum mechanics (see Stephen Hawking, David Bohm, David Peate, and Ken Wilber for examples).

Therapy is still based almost entirely on this classical, linear model of particle science (see Victor Vernon Woolf, Ken Wilber, David Peate and David Bohm). Most scientists now agree that reality is both "particle" and "wave." Few yet realize that reality is also "conscious." The human body is likewise both particle and wave and few would argue against the conscious nature of the body.

Our atoms, microtubules, neurons and brain stem, are composed of multiple life forms that are living in symbiosis. These microsystems give form to our organs and body. They can better be understood when explored on quantum and consciousness principles. Since the physical universe is, in some dimension of reality, conscious and quantum, therapy must also be viewed as the quantum exploration of conscious reality.

CHAPTER TWO

THE MULTIPLE DIMENSIONS OF THERAPY

*T*HE MULTIPLE DIMENSIONS OF THERAPY

8. The Full Potential Self - "our counterpart in hyperspace"

Particles, as in photons and atoms, have a counterpart in hyperspace. Likewise people have a counterpart in hyperspace.[1, 2, 8]

In the quantum dimension, this "potential self" of each person on earth is inseparably connected to the entire microsystem of the body. The physical person is a holographic projection of its fullest potential self (herein called "The Full Potential Self").

In quantum biology, the Full Potential Self is described as "pre-computing spinner networks of information systems in hyperspace." From this view of reality, each person and each situation in which we find ourselves is "driven by potential." All personal choice is pre-computed in hyperspace. Accessing the Full Potential Self is not only helpful, but is vital to the therapy process. Of all the discoveries of modern science, the discovery of the Full Potential Self is perhaps the most beneficial to human development.

9. Multidimensional definitions of "Self"

The holodynamic definition of "Self" includes: definitions of Self that exist in space-time (as in the Ego Self); definitions of self that are hyperspacial Self (as in the Full Potential Self) and those definitions of Self that come from various holodynes.[9]

Holodynes affect one's consciousness, including one's self-definitions. Addressing anything less than the entire network of self-definitions diminishes the individual and thus diminishes the effectiveness of therapy.

In therapy, the introduction of the Full Potential Self can produce a primary reference that calls into alignment any disharmony, dysfunction or expression that is less than its full potential. This alignment stimulates extra-ordinary therapeutic movement.

Holodynes that attempt to impose their own self-definitions can be recognized, accessed and transformed (assisted to unfold their fullest potential). All dimensions of reality are, according to the best information available, "created equal." Thus all definitions of self contain potential that equally seeks manifestation.

Therapy becomes the process of transforming and integrating the various definitions of Self so their potential can be aligned with that of the Full Potential Self.

10. The "primary reference" for individual therapy is personal potential

The Full Potential Self is the primary reference for individual therapy.[10] The full Potential Self is "pre-computing" each set of circumstances for the individual. This perspective includes those holodynes that are causing behavioral problems in a person's life. Holodynes that are dysfunctional and causing problems are immature. Like all life forms, they want to "grow up" or to reach their potential.

The challenge of therapy is for the individual to tap into the menu of options from the Full Potential Self and choose to unfold the potential of their holodynes. This process, of potentializing holodynes, permits the field of information to be transformed. This transformation can create a quantum alignment with the Full Potential Self and open the door for personal coherence. The primary reference for personal therapy is the identification of personal potential for all information systems. Once identified, this potential can be unfolded.

11. "I" am always bigger than "my problem

One of the gifts of the therapist is to be able to recognize the potential that drives each person and situation in life. Every problem becomes an invitation to unfold potential and create coherence.[11] Therapy provides an environment where the "real me" is recognized in relationship to problems. The person's "I" is larger than any "problem."

The process of labeling or diagnosing people with some hidden language that labels them as "sick" or "mentally ill" or in need of treatment is not therapy. Exploring what potential drives the "set of circumstances" that created the identified problem is the beginning of therapy. Knowing the potential that drives each of us as a person, drives our actions, or drives our thoughts and emotions and what potential is the "real me" that drives everything else about a person's life, is therapy.

People, relationships, families and community systems cannot be put in a box and confined to a specific treatment plan. Reality is dynamic, not static. Therapy reflects a changing universe with flexible changes in perspective. This dynamic approach allows each person to understand that each problem is, in some dimension, chosen so that the solution can be manifest. From this view, each person is, in reality, larger than any problem he or she may be facing.

12. Relationship therapy references the "Being Of Togetherness"

Each relationship has a network of holodynes that manages and controls it. We have come to refer to this network as the "Being of Togetherness" (BOT). [12] Understanding the BOT unveils a collective consciousness that literally "manages" each relationship.

Accessing the dimension of the BOT produces remarkable personal growth and therapeutic movement in relationships. When the primary focus of relationship therapy is the fullest potential of the relationship, this focus shifts the state of consciousness of the therapist and of the participants to the dimension in which the relationship has its own consciousness. Every relationship, like every person, is unique and dynamic. Take, for example, family therapy.

When therapy focuses on the information systems that control family dynamics, maximum therapeutic movement results in minimum time. Such movement is quantum. It includes individual and couple therapy while maintaining family growth. Similar movement can be evidenced in systems of all kinds, including religious and government systems. Part of the public trust awarded to therapists is that the therapy process will afford the primary experience of unfolding of the fullest life potential of individuals, relationships, families, groups and systems. In this process, participants hope to experience reality and learn about living principles and universal consciousness.

This approach does not require the therapist to take charge of anyone's life, make decisions for another, or take control of anyone. Focusing on collective networks makes it possible to walk with people and facilitate their search for the deep reservoir of their own potential. It does not, however, work when a therapist "plays God." Just as therapy works best in collaboration, using the Full Potential Self as the primary reference of personal therapy, likewise it is also evident that collective therapy works best by encouraging self-organization and potentialization of solutions for relationships and systems at every level of consciousness. Therapy works from micro to macro based upon the same principles.

FOOTNOTES - CHAPTER TWO

8. The hyperspacial "counterpart" — the Full Potential Self: The existence of hyperspace, zero-point energy, the quantum potential field and the activity of spinners of information giving form to physical reality, has led to the discovery that everything has a hyperspacial counterpart.

When these findings are applied to human beings, the reality of each person's counterpart gives a personal reference to work done with holographics, subatomic physics, black holes, gravity and multidimensional mathematics that attempt to explain the nature of reality.

In subatomic physics, counterparts are used to explain antimatter and antiparticles. Each type of matter exists as part of the balancing effect of the universe and, when they collide, they turn into pure energy. When the holographic principle is applied to something like a black hole, an extra two dimensions become available by which black holes can be better understood (see Stephen Hawking, *The Universe in a Nutshell*, 2001). The concept of a "Full Potential Self" emerged from the practice of therapy in which most people are able to access their personal "counterpart" as a "being of light" or some similar representation that contains real and valuable information used in the solution to complex problems. This ability to access one's personal hyperspacial counterpart has produced extraordinary results in therapeutic movement (see Woolf 1990, 2005).

9. Therapy embraces multidimensional definitions of "Self": In order to explain the forces of gravity that are evident in space, scientists have uncovered an invisible world of antimatter. This enfolded dimension of reality is at least equal in mass to the mass of the entire universe and some contend that it may constitute more than 97 percent of physical reality. In some writings, this matter is referred to as hyperspace, or dark matter, because it cannot be seen by the human eye.

Within the dimension of hyperspace is what Hawking describes as each person's hyperspacial counterpart. It is postulated that our hyperspacial counterpart is a *5-brane* (or more) complex being (*p=5 branes* or above – meaning a being that encompasses more dimensions or *p-branes* than space and time). What appears to be the best definition available is that this multidimensional being is "projecting onto our holographic world" the image of itself. This image shows up, for example, as a person. I call this hyperspacial multidimensional person the "Full Potential Self.

Beyond the theoretical conjectures, the actual conscious focus on the Full Potential Self produces extraordinary therapeutic results. It can bring new, valid information, insights, added strength, meaning, and a host of other ingredients that add to therapeutic movement. See, V. Vernon Woolf, *Holodynamics: How to Manage your Personal Power*, 1990 or Stephen Hawking *The Universe in a Nutshell*. The primary Self is the Full Potential Self.

There are many other sources of self-definition. These sources arise from the enfolded holographic dimension of consciousness. Self-organizing information systems can be inherited;

modeled for us by family, friends and cultural influences; created by our own imaginations; or tranceived from parallel worlds. No matter what the source, these information systems are stored within the microtubules as "holodynes" (see note 15 below). Holodynes contain multiple definitions of self, each with the power to cause, and each with limited maturity.

10. My "primary reference" for therapy is my Full Potential Self: Information organizes according to sets of circumstances that exhibit bounded parameters called "event horizons." The problems people have are contained within specific event horizons. When the person's consciousness is focused from within the event horizon, the person's senses and perception are limited to information within the event horizon and thus solutions are often difficult to find. It is a widely accepted consensus that moving one's focus (from "inside" the problem to "outside" the problem, for example) is helpful in solving the problem. Information theory and certain therapy schools of thought have established the custom of avoiding "transference" or becoming too involved "in" the client's problem. But, when the person is able to "step out of the problem" and "observe" it, especially through the eyes of one's fullest potential, therapy is accelerated.

The process of "stepping out of the problem" is another way of saying "shift one's reference to outside of the event horizon of holodynes that are causing the problem." When one's primary reference is centered within the event horizon of one's Full Potential Self, it becomes possible to access any information necessary for solving problems. We have learned from years of testing that the Full Potential Self represents the potential that drives every set of circumstances. Information from the Full Potential Self is capable of pre-computations that allow for freedom of choice. (See Woolf, *Dance of Life*, 2005).

11. 'I' am always bigger than my "problem": It is suggested that some dimension or p-brane exists beyond the normal experience of the situation and can be accessed to potentialize solutions to problems. (See footnotes 1-10 above). It also points out that a p=4 brane view (four-dimensional consciousness of space-time) does not represent the complete picture of reality. Individuals are not limited to the dimensions being measured by the physical senses and neither is therapy.

The "I" of each person may be composed of at least 11 dimensions. Similarly, the "problem" of a person may be the result of a limited scope of consciousness and can always be "overcome" by increasing one's scope by including another view of the situation from a more expanded view of reality. Every school of thought regarding therapy agrees, more or less, with this approach (Woolf 1990).

12. Relationship therapy references the "Being of Togetherness": The Being of Togetherness refers to the fullest potential for the relationship (see "Field-shifting" by Woolf, 2006, for specifics as to the nature of the holodynes that control relationships). Such holodynes are complex, include ideal images, inherited and multidimensional dynamics, and account for finding the solutions to relationship challenges.

CHAPTER THREE

THERAPY AS THE TRANSFORMATION OF INFORMATION

*T*HERAPY AS THE *T*RANSFORMATION OF *I*NFORMATION

13. Therapy is the transformation of information

Everything is made of information. In this conscious universe, information cannot be lost or destroyed. *It can only be changed in form.*[13]

Once the therapist discovers that everything is made of information, it becomes possible to explore people's lives as being part of a conscious universe where past memories, alternative histories or parallel worlds can be transformed or *changed in form.* It becomes evident that muting of memory has short-lived benefits. It will simply return. If you try to release the information, you only invite it to "re-lease" or "take out another lease" on time spent with its host. Therapy is the transformation of information.

Hyperspacial information "spinners" give form to matter and are an integral part of a person's well-being. When influences create misinformation, it forms into holodynes that can block the connection to our hyperspacial, quantum or physical reality. Therapy has the opportunity to explore what creates these blocks and how to access their various dimensions at their source. It is a learning process whereby people learn how to transform their holodynes, to reconnect and realign with their Full Potential Self and thus re-establish their sense of mental health. Therapy can literally change the form of reality, past, present and future.

14. Therapy identifies, explores and transforms holodynes

The therapist can be more objective than the person caught up in problems. The therapist understands people are not their holodynes. It is possible for the therapist to work from outside the influence of holodynes and observe them as information systems that have become self-organized and developed causal potency.[14] The therapist can look at the self-perpetuating power, the ability of holodynes to cause things to happen (and make sure they keep on happening) and facilitate the transformation of such holodynes. The negative things, all the "crazy making," violence, war, crime, humankind's inhumanity, disease and mental imbalance can be transformed. At the same time, some holodynes are neutral and some also have great strength and demonstrate qualities that are of therapeutic value, so the therapy process explores which holodynes are to be maintained and which need to be transformed.

15. Therapy follows the implicate order

From a quantum perspective, reality manifests according to an implicate or "built-in" order. This implicate order forms the basic laws by which life manifests.[15] When we apply the implicate order to consciousness, there is a built-in order by which we grow into the well-being of our fullest potential. Therapy provides the opportunity to explore the basic patterns wherein consciousness emerges and how growth takes place, and to experience how maturity develops step by step through various stages of development.

In each dimension, there is an order. Holodynes, for example, are quantum and follow a similar implicate order to that followed in the growth of humans. Such therapy moves beyond classifications, confinement programs, drug prescriptions and electro-shock treatments. Therapy explores all dimensions of consciousness, options, holodynes, transformation procedures and the implicate order by which people come into well-being. Therapy helps people take their next natural step in the implicate order of their own growth. One of the options is to access people's holodynes and facilitate their transformation through the built-in order of their own growth so they can apply this new state of being in the next step of their own development. This is therapy. Not that other stuff.

FOOTNOTES - CHAPTER THREE

13. Therapy is the transformation of information: The laws of conservation of energy suggest that energy cannot be lost or destroyed. It can only be changed in form. Heat from a stove, for example, is not lost. It transforms (changes its form) and heats the air or any other object close enough to absorb the heat. This energy can be turned to steam that can be used to run a steam engine. This same law of conservation applies to all forms of energy.

Energy is made of information in motion. Therefore, information obeys the same laws of conservation. This can be evidenced, for example, in a black hole where everything is absorbed and nothing escapes. But, when the holographic principle is applied to black holes, the information that is absorbed can be viewed as "stored for release" into "other dimensions" not visible to ordinary senses. (See Hawking, 2001).

In therapy, holodynes causing downdraft dynamics cannot be repressed or destroyed. They invariably turn up in some other dimension of life, sometimes skipping generations to appear at a later time. Once transformed, however, they give no evidence of showing up in another dimension because they have a field of manifestation in updraft circumstances (Woolf, 1990, 2005, 2006).

14. Therapy identifies, explores and transforms holodynes: Consciousness has an enfolded dimension: the dimension of holodynes. While the entire matrix of physical reality appears to be holographic, specific information systems found within the microtubules of every cell seem to be specifically designed to store holodynes.

Information is input into this dimension from sensory sources of the body and environment. It can also come from hyperspacial or parallel dimensions. Information is stored in multidimensional forms that have "the power to cause" (called "holodynes," meaning "whole units of power").

Holodynes self-organize. They develop through stages of an implicate order, which includes the ability to preserve themselves, send and receive information, develop relationships with other holodynes and cause things to happen. They are "causal" in the field of consciousness. Holodynes are inherited, pass on from generation to generation, and are able to "imbed themselves" in the collective consciousness. When a holodyne is not fully developed, or "immature," it can cause imbalance and chaos in a person's life.

Holodynes imbedded within the collective can cause war, ignorance and every other form of inhuman behavior. One of the primary services offered by therapy is to consciously identify holodynes, explore the information they contain, and transform them for the benefit of the individual and the collective. This process is called "Tracking" in Holodynamic Therapy. (See Woolf, 1990, 1994, and Rector 1996).

15. Therapy follows the implicate order: See, for example, David Bohm's concepts in his book *Wholeness and the Implicate Order*. This controversial work suggests that everything grows according to a built-in order. While this order can be seen in the mathematics and geometry of all living things, it does not imply determinism. On the contrary, it seems to work as a mechanism for the emerging of different levels of consciousness that are orchestrating a complex ordered matrix of information in various dimensions that form matter and life. Such an order would also apply to human consciousness. See, for example, Piaget, Kohlberg and Woolf. Therapy, in order to be maximally effective, would follow the implicate order of therapy. More than three decades of research have already gone into the search for this order. The processes of "Tracking," "Reliving" and "Preliving" are examples of therapeutic processes that follow the implicate order. Associated with these are processes known as "Place of Peace," "Full Potential Self," "Potentializing," "Place of Planning," and others (see Woolf, 1990, 2005, Rector 1996).

CHAPTER FOUR

THERAPY IS SELF-INITIATED

*T*HERAPY IS *S*ELF-*I*NITIATED

16. Therapy promotes self-initiated change

Information systems stabilize and grow naturally when change is self-initiated.[16] Therapy makes available the choice to self-Track and self-transform holodynes. People can learn to do this for themselves as part of their right to self-transformation. They can access, befriend and feed in new information to their holodynes so they can transform into their fullest potential. Therapy promotes this kind of transformation as a self-initiated process of potentialization. It brings the holodyne into quantum coherence with our own Full Potential Self. This alignment process is each person's responsibility. The therapist cannot do it for another. Each person, no matter what he or she may have been taught, is capable. Trust is a two-way street in therapy. Therapy promotes self-initiated change.

17. Therapy creates a menu of options

To align with the Full Potential Self is to open a menu of options without the limits of time or space.[17] Therapy is an opportunity to facilitate a more conscious experience of accessing, communicating with, forming an alliance – an alignment - with all aspects of reality. Holodynamic therapy can help restore memory, unveil options, explore choices, empower self-initiation and manage responsibility.

Therapy reinforces trust in self, in the therapy relationship, and in society. Therapy fosters trust in life. People who seek therapy seek solutions and often what they seek can only be found in those dimensions of consciousness that are enfolded within our reality. It is often within these enfolded dimensions that participants discover their options and therapy offers the opportunity to explore one's inherent menu of options.

18. Therapy facilitates choice

Consciousness is a state of being from which people become more able to "collapse" their menu of options into specific form. They can do this because, woven into the fabric of time and space, is the "causal potency" of free-will choice.[18] Therapy provides an environment that can be safe and supportive while encouraging the expression of free will. It not only increases awareness of the menu of options, but provides the freedom to make choices as the experience of therapy. People become aware of their options and take responsibility for what is best for their well-being.

This process may require focusing beyond the limitations of rational thinking or emotional dynamics. It requires providing the opportunity for accessing any relevant dimension of reality, including hyperspacial and quantum information fields, wherein people exist in a state of being capable of choice. Therapy facilitates the availability of choice and the exercise of free will.

19. Therapy is self-organizing

Information systems are self-organizing.[19] This means people want a therapist who is dynamic, well-informed and active rather than a person who is passive, does nothing, suggests nothing, and just reflects back to them their own endless dialogues.

The therapist provides an environment wherein the conditions of self-organization can be met. That includes *having sufficient information, energy and non-linear flexibility* so that self-organization can take place. These are the environmental conditions by which life self-organizes, and therapy can offer nothing less.

20. Therapy is self-realizing

The presence of a therapist goes beyond techniques and theory. Like the process of therapy, the therapist must be multidimensional – holodynamic.[20] Central to the therapy process is the process of self-realization. Unlike computers, people are self-aware. Therapy helps expand this self-awareness into our own daily consciousness.

Therapy probes the parts of consciousness that have become "comfortable," "invisible" or even "malfunctional" and yet are empowered within the various dimensions of consciousness. Therapy facilitates self-realization. It opens our eyes to views beyond our closed event horizons about our hidden realities and facilitates self-realization.

21. Therapy is committed to self-initiated action

The essence of free will of a person is bonded to action. The options available from the Full Potential Self and pre-cognitive choices in hyperspace set the stage for action in daily situations.[21] Therapy acknowledges this entanglement and facilitates the experience of inner alignment and action in daily life.

"Action" includes involvement with processes as in establishing a "Place of Peace," daily communication with one's "Full Potential Self," creating a "Round Table" for conferencing with one's holodynes, and the conscious use of the "Place of Planning" to gain information.

Therapy is committed to the creation of self-initiated action that utilizes each dimension of consciousness.

FOOTNOTES - CHAPTER FOUR

16. Therapy promotes self-initiated change: One of the definitions of "life" is "self-initiative action." Therapy promotes life-generating processes and thus, by definition, therapy promotes self-initiated action.

17. Therapy creates a menu of options: See Roger Penrose's "Shadows of the Mind" for "pre-computed" information networks that create a menu of options prior to conscious choice.

18. Therapy facilitates choice: From the holographic dimension of hyperspace, the Full Potential Self (see footnote 10 above) is involved in "pre-computing networks of information in motion" that "create a menu of options" for any given situation here in this space-time continuum (see Penrose). In other words, "choice is!" Therapy responds to reality, i.e., what is.

19. Therapy is self-organizing: Information theory has identified certain information systems, such as are "superposition's," in which quantum computers can maintain polarizations (such as "on" and "off") at the same time.

Quantum computer also exhibit self-organizing qualities. Such systems can, for example, maintain, adjust and seem to "learn" from their experiences, are able to "reset" themselves with complex information fields, conduct trillions of computations per second, and operate without the use of energy input. Such systems are referred to as "self-organizing" (see "Holodynamics and Quantum Computer Models" by Woolf and Blue, 2001, on the Internet. Go to www.holodynamics.com/articles).

Human intelligence operates upon quantum principles that are much more complex than quantum computers, and it is self-evident that human consciousness is self-organizing. The reference to having sufficient information, energy and non-linear flexibility is taken from a Nobel Prize winner's work on the "primal soup" requirements for forming life (see Prigogene). Ilya Prigogene's work on self-organizing systems was instrumental in opening the doorway to a different way of thinking about the life of natural systems.

Prigogene understood that systems could reconstitute at a higher level of complexity and keep on going. New, improved, and better able to deal with a changed environment, these systems just seemed to pop into a new way of being. Systems of all sorts went on a journey which began in order, passed through chaos, then ended in new order - indeed a vastly improved new order. Many credit Prigogene's work as the beginning of Chaos and Complexity Theory. This entire field of study is groundwork for therapists.

20. Therapy is self-realizing: While this statement may be self-evident, the principles and processes of self-realization, along with many references, may be found in *The Holodynamic State of Being: the Advocate Manual*, Woolf, 2005. See also footnote 19.

21. Therapy is committed to self-initiated action: Refer to footnote 20 above for the processes of "Place of Peace," "Full Potential Self," and "Tracking." For the ""Re-live"" and "P"Re-live"" processes, refer to *Presence in a Conscious Universe: the Consultant's Manual,* Woolf, 2005. Also refer to *Field Shifting: Orders within Orders of Consciousness and the Holodynamic Integration,* Woolf, 2006.

CHAPTER FIVE

THERAPY PROCESSES

_T_HERAPY _PROCESSES_

22. Therapy advocates equality

The therapist walks beside people, not in front of them, and not behind them. People are equal to their opportunities to grow, learn and heal themselves. Like the dimensions of physical reality in science, all dimensions of consciousness are created equal.[22] The public trust holds that the therapist will never violate this equality, lord it over people, or treat them like "specimens." Therapists will not deny people their basic human rights to speak their truth, protect themselves, or learn for themselves. Therapy advocates equality.

23. Therapy is not bound by time

Time is relative to its dimension of consciousness. In hyperspace time has a shape and turns back in upon itself. Computations, done in that domain, await an invitation to manifest into physical form. This "awaiting" state is referred to as "the quantum state of a potential field." It is, hypothetically, a state of possibilities. The corresponding choice of possibilities manifests here in space and time.[23]

When we make a choice, for example, our own conscious choice collapses the hyperspacial quantum field of options into a specific form within a specific time. This process appears instantaneous. When this process is applied to therapy, it is evident that it does not require years of therapy to experience a new state of being. Gone are the days of permanent lodging for the mentally ill. Gone are the days of the 50-minute hour for therapy sessions. Therapy cannot be dictated by the clock.

Therapeutic movement occurs outside of the boundaries of time. Change occurs by choice in alliance with hyperspacial information fields involving the Full Potential Self of the person who is participating. No matter what their situation in life, people cannot be contained in an unlimited cocoon woven with the threads of time. Therapy gets them out of their confined limitations as soon as possible.

24. Therapeutic dimensions rise beyond linear or physical models

Mental health cannot be limited to a linear or physical model because consciousness is not limited to the physical brain or neural pathways of the body. Nor can consciousness be limited to what is going on in the microtubules. Microtubules contain an encased environment to protect and create complex expressions of consciousness (tubulin walls made of valence-varying dimer molecules). They are structured so as to be capable of organizing, storing and sustaining complex information as holographic networked information systems.[24] The aquatic environment of the microtubules is surrounded by valence-positioned dimer switches on the tubulin walls. While this entire system is central to consciousness, it functions as a conduit for information exchange with other dimensions, such as the hyperspacial dimension.

Once the therapist recognizes that all physical forms are hyperspacially connected, the therapy process moves beyond the limitations of temporal body organs or mechanistic organic processes. Therapy is more than chemotherapy. Therapy models must encompass all mechanisms of consciousness and all the dimensions to which consciousness is connected.

Likewise, the consciousness of the therapist extends beyond temporal models. Therapy holds the possibility of states of being beyond the limits of time and space. Therapy provides an environment so people can create coherence and well-being.

25. Therapy helps create a state of being at peace

Reality sustains an internal harmonic state of being wherein all information exhibits coherence. Humans, however, often produce apparent lack of coherence. This disharmony is found in every type of personal and social conflict. Therapy provides a setting in which each person and/or group can re-establish their internal harmonic state of being or "Place of Peace." A Place of Peace can be imaginary or it can be the reflection of some past event in which a person was "at peace." [25]

To be conscious of one's Place of Peace is to create an environment outside of all the conflicts of life. It establishes a safe, internal atmosphere from which all information can be processed in a more conscious, effective manner. People often create a "Round Table," or internal meeting place, from which they can orchestrate more conscious control over their internal dynamics.

26. Therapy accesses the holographic dimension of holodynes

One of the most fascinating dimensions of therapy is the holographic dimension. Consciousness is holographic. Holographic screens cover all human senses. [1,26] Neural messages are transmitted in holographic language. All thoughts and feelings are stored in holographic form. These holographic forms are called "holodynes," or "whole units of power," because they have "the power to cause." It is possible to access holodynes. Holodynes are self-organizing information systems stored within the microtubules of all living cells.

Microtubules are small, thread-like tubes that make up the fabric of cells, neurons and other body organs. Microtubules are filled with ionic pure water. In this protected environment, holodynes can be observed to grow, give off specific information, and maintain control on body and mental functions. When we apply an anesthetic to the microtubules, all consciousness stops. Information stored within the holodynes becomes blocked. Blocked holodynes can cause body functions to break down; then we experience "dis-ease" and our body processes begin to malfunction. When we block the holodynes controlling our mental process, psychological well-being becomes incoherent. All health conditions depend upon healthy holodynes.

There are many influences that can block or inhibit information from our holodynes – even conflicting information from other holodynes. This conflicting information must be integrated in order to restore health and well-being. In order to do this, one must transform the blocked holodynes.

In order to transform holodynes, one must access the holodynes, communicate with them, find their potential, and help them align with that potential. The result of this alignment is transformational. This "change in form" results in a restoration of quantum coherence that produces a morphogenic field – a growing environment – for health. This transforming of information systems is the primal activity of therapy. Applying therapy processes to the dimension of holodynes creates changes in every dimension of consciousness, including the healing of the body and mind. Transformation of holodynes is essential to mental health.[26]

27. The transformation of emotions through "Tracking"

Another dimension of therapy allows the conscious transformation of emotions. Emotions are holographic and, in this dimension of reality, are contained within a specific event horizon as holodynes. Holodynes transmit their information and their influence through the neural system, causing both thoughts and feelings. People who are diagnosed according to a DMIV classification (the official mental illness diagnostic manual for psychotherapists), for example, are seen as exhibiting emotional and mental "dysfunction," which is the classification we put upon immature holodynes.

Mental illness is a state of being caused by holodynes. [1, 27] This state of being can be transformed by transforming the holodynes that are "causing" it. This process of accessing and transforming the holodynes is called "tracking." Tracking allows each holodyne to experience its own natural growth according to an implicate order by which it matures. When properly experienced, tracking allows a change of the state of being of the holodynes within the person and the result is that the symptoms of dysfunction disappear.[27] Transformation of holodynes is essential to emotional health.

28. Shifting collective consciousness through the "Re-live/Pre-live" processes

Collective consciousness has to do with individual holodynes that communicate hyperspacially to others in a family or group. This ability is referred to as "swarm intelligence" in nature and is found in the swarm behaviors of bees, flocks of birds, schools of fish, and other species. Because their communication is hyperspacial (faster than the speed of light), those involved perceive and move as a collective.

The information controlling swarm behavior is transmitted directly from within the microtubule *portals*. Thus, within each species, the microtubules contain quantum portals capable of instant communication. It appears instant because it takes place without the passage of normal time. People have this same ability. They can often sense information *as a group* and act upon it without apparent prior thought. Many of our problems are the result of our collective, subconscious, swarm activity.[28]

Therapy provides a safe environment to explore how the human dimensions of collective consciousness work and what to do about it when we become the victims of collective malfunction or imbalance. The process of pre-living allows an individual or group to access information from the past, transform it and integrate it with the present. The situations are, in reality, "re-lived."

In a similar fashion, information from the future can be accessed and "pre-lived" so that coherence can be established with the present. Therapy applies to everyone, both the individual and the collective community. To change a single holodyne holds the potential for changing the entire collective.

29. Potentialization

Our microtubule portals send information into hyperspace. Since everything is made of information in motion, these quantum potential portals hold immeasurable potential for transformation of both space and time. These portals contain the mechanisms for our connection to our hyperspacial counterparts and pollinate the seeds of consciousness that can transform both space and time.[29]

From this dimension we can influence the holographics of nature and understand the whole dynamic of a conscious universe. We have come to call this process "potentialization." Using what is known allows a natural progressive path toward unfolding potential. It also indicates that, when we change a single holodyne, the change process holds the potential for changing the nature of the physical universe. Therefore, therapy holds forth the possibility of unlimited change.

30. Our "bond" with the past and future

Since mass and energy are directly related to velocity (Einstein), and since space and time are relative, time has a "shape" (Hawking). It can turn back upon itself.[30]

In this dimension of consciousness, the past and future are running parallel to the present. Since everything is conscious, scientists have raised the question as to whether we can actually travel into the past or future. A "Star Trek" mentality has arisen in which information and everything we are experiencing is proposed as *inseparably* bounded to our past and future.

We can think faster than the speed of light. We are also innately capable of being conscious of the whole dynamic, past, present and future. When therapy is recognized as a hyper-spacial communication process, the therapy process cannot be confined to any specific segment of time. Each person is inseparably connected to the past and future. Thus events of the past or future can be transformed as part of the therapy process. This "breakthrough" into the past and future has resulted in the solution to many of the most difficult problems in therapy.

FOOTNOTES - CHAPTER FIVE

22. Therapy advocates equality: Refer to *Field Shifting: The Holodynamics of integration: Manual III*, Woolf, 2006. This manual discusses in some detail the solution to the games of dominance, including the effects that occur when one person seeks to diminish another. (See also *The Dance of Life*, Woolf, 2005).

23. Therapy is not bound by time: Stephen Hawking (2001) suggests that time, like light, "bends back upon itself." In addition, he shows the "holographic" view of time. "Time," he says, "has shape." He shows a representation of the shape of time as a great mobius loop. For those "caught" in the dimension of time, time always appears to be one-directional. The implications of this discovery become evident in the therapy process when participants access dimensions of consciousness that carry them beyond the confines of time. They can then access any given period of time. In a conscious state of being, they can travel backward or forward in time. Thus the therapy process is not limited by old views of time but incorporates these new findings into the therapy processes.

24. Therapeutic dimensions rise beyond linear or physical models: This is an adaptation of a quote from David Bohm's original book, *Science and the Implicate Order*. "Reality cannot be contained within a linear model." See footnotes 1-13 above. Consciousness cannot be contained within a linear model. Nor can it be confined to physical dimensions. See, *The Dance of Life*, Woolf, 2005

25. The Place of Peace: A harmonic state of being that can be triggered by imagining a place in which all conflict and/or distractions do not exist (see Woolf, 1990).

26. Holodynes: Holodynes are inherited, modeled by family and culture, come from parallel dimensions or form as part of the creative nature of consciousness (see *Holodynamics*, Woolf, 1990). Information that goes into the making of a holodyne can come from any or all of these various sources. Inherited holodynes, for example, are carried via microtubules. The sperm and egg both contain vast amount of potential information within their microtubules. The memory of the entire human race could, theoretically, be included in the holodyne matrix within a single microtubule. It is like asking, "How many waves are there in the ocean?"

Studies on split twins, disease predisposition and cultural and transgenerational patterning, have all raised the question: "Is it inherited or environmental?" In reality, it is both and a lot more. In one sense, holodynes are the "most-likely-to-survive" dimension of the human race. Not only are they woven into the fabric of the body, the cells, neurons and organs, but they are modeled and reinforced by intimate family and friends, culture and society from birth onward through life. There is ample evidence to demonstrate that holodynes also come from parallel worlds. There appear to be many p-brane dimensions involved in the world of holodynes. Almost as if we wanted to make it more interesting, we can also change our holodynes, create new ones or transform old ones, get new information from parallel worlds and pass the holodynes on to the next generation (refer to Woolf, 1990, 2005, and 2006).

27. Transformation of holodynes transforms emotions through "Tracking": All information systems work according to a similar implicate order. Transformation takes place as the necessary information required for each stage of development is provided. (See footnotes 15 and 16 above. Also see Woolf 1990, 2005, or Rector 1996). Emotions follow patterns that are typically non-linear. Like waves, they have no beginning or end (refer to, *Principle-Driven Transformation: the Holodynamics of the Dance of Life*, Woolf, 2006, or Woolf, 1990).

28. The Dimension of collective consciousness and the "Re-live" and "Pre-live" processes: Collective consciousness or "swarm intelligence" and how it affects our psychological well-being began with Carl Jung's early works on psychology and his innumerable following both in the practice of therapy and in the theoretical developments. But this school of thought also includes work from information theory, as in Kevin Kelly's *Out of Control.* Kelly indicates there is clear evidence that species such as birds, insects and fish all demonstrate the ability to communicate hyperspacially, faster than can be measured. These documented facts are included in the holodynamic approach to therapy. People demonstrate this ability to sense things collectively - beyond the limits of time. Consciousness can be "sent" via Frohlech frequencies to others. This accounts for collective consciousness in groups and in society. See Kelly, Jung, Woolf and related footnotes.

29. Therapy can change the physics of the universe: physical reality and "potentialization": Theoretically, this world is contained within a 4-brane hologram that has a "one-to-one relationship" with hyperspace and its multidimensional realms (refer to Hawking, 2001, page 198). In light of this, combined with the probability of parallel universes co-existing within the same space as our universe, or in parallel with it, it is theoretically consistent to suppose that consciousness "rules." That is, when one's conscious self is aligned with one's hyperspacial, Full Potential Self, a menu of options is opened. A single choice here, in this reality, could very well be influencing what is referred to as "the collapse of the wave" in a quantum world. From the menu of all possibilities, that possibility which becomes "real," or manifest in this space-time continuum, is precipitated by our conscious choice. The process of creation is going on in our present time (Wolf, Fred Alan, 1995 and Woolf, Victor Vernon, 2005).

30. The dimension beyond time and our "bond" with the past and future: From a quantum perspective, everything is connected in some dimension of reality. John Wheeler's *Many Worlds Interpretation of Quantum Mechanics* made clear the consistency of the multiple-worlds approach to reality, and physicists like Stephen Hawking have made it clear that time, like light, bends. From a beyond-time perspective, the past and the future are running in parallel with the present. This perspective makes sense when it is applied to the science of consciousness. (See Woolf, 2005; Hawking, 2001)

CHAPTER SIX

BIOLOGICAL ASPECTS OF THERAPY

BIOLOGICAL ASPECTS OF THERAPY

31. The dimension of hyperspace and our DNA

From our linear heritage, we have come to believe that we inherit some of those traits we believe limit our lives. "It's in our DNA," we say. Yet, our hyperspacial connection can be observed in the formation of DNA.

As the DNA molecule grows, two perfectly correlated spinners appear and help guide the growth of the protein strings that form the double helix loop. There is one spinner for each of the strands as they grow into their exact position. The spinners also direct the forming of the bridge and, then, when that specific section of the DNA strand is completed, two more spinners appear at the points where the growth must continue. This spinner activity continues until the entire DNA coil is finished.[31]

Similar "spinner" activity appears within the microtubules, making possible the formation of holodynes. The DNA and the microtubules reflect classical, quantum and holodynamic phenomenon acting in coherence and manifesting consciousness at various stages of its emergence. Inherited characteristics, long thought to be deterministic, originate in hyperspace. They are part of the information network that is linked to choice. Therapy reflects a dynamic universe, in which the DNA and inherited characteristics are made of dynamic information systems and open to choice and to change and subject to therapy.

32. Unlimited energy

In computer-generated cybernetic models, single strands of water molecules can be seen spinning out from the outer edge of the quantum potential field. Physics teaches us that these single strands are capable of transmitting both information and energy in either direction ("inward" from the holodynes, or "outward" from the quantum potential field). This means that both energy and information are available from hyperspace. According to quantum physics, there is an "unlimited" amount of energy within a quantum potential field.[32]

Therapy reflects the possibility that people have access, in some dimension of consciousness, to such unlimited energy. Therapy moves us out of our private world of deprivation and into the universal possibility of unlimited energy.

33. Unfolding personal and collective potential

In a quantum world, everything is driven by potential. [33] When this principle is applied to therapy, problems are viewed as solutions waiting to unfold. Those who have forgotten their connection with conscious reality have blocked the unfolding of their potential. When the therapist labels the person as "patient" and gives them a "classification," it may be deemed necessary in order to collect insurance, but the process of classification can be counterproductive. It tends to make the "person" a "problem. People may submit to labels and administrative justifications but they will resist every effort to disconnect them from their personal holodynamic reality.

Therapy is a personal remembering for each and a recalling process, an opportunity to reconnect with their hyperspacial, quantum Self and with their multidimensional world. The therapist is invited into the process of remembering because people relate to their therapist. This connection is Full-Potential-Self to Full-Potential-Self and reaches beyond space and time. There is a kind of therapeutic "magic" in the personal exchange when people reconnect to their "I am" and include the therapist. Therapy becomes a "we are" experience, an alignment process that reflects the synergy of unfolding potential. The therapy process can reflect this magic and provide an environment directed toward the unfolding of potential. This "connection" can include relationships with others, or couples, or family therapy or collective therapy, when we choose to unfold our potential together.

FOOTNOTES - CHAPTER SIX

30. Therapy is bonded to the past and future: See footnote 23 for an explanation of the holographic nature of time. Also review footnote 27 on collective consciousness. For those who have followed the information as outline above, it becomes obvious that all information, including time itself, is interrelated. For those who study human behavior, it is also obvious that people are often "ruled" by the past or "driven" by the future. The actual "impact" of the past and future upon daily living is the subject of many books. We are all "bonded" to our past and our future. Not only can we "think" about it, or "sense" the field in which we experience life, but we can "access" beyond time and consciously "enter" the past and/or future. The therapist recognizes these dimensions of reality and utilizes them in the therapy process. For details, see Woolf, Penrose, and Rector.

31. Therapy influences our DNA: Another one of those "best-kept secrets" in science is the role played by "spinners." While it is generally accepted that everything is made of information in motion and that all atoms are best described as "standing waves," the general public is less aware of the essential role played by "spinners." According to world scholar Karl Pribram, the DNA coil grows under direct control of spinners. He describes how two spinners appear from out of the quantum potential field at precisely the points where the protein strings (that are forming the DNA double-helix coil) need to grow. Once the molecular growth has taken place, the "bridge" string then forms between the two spinners and they are replaced by two more spinners – now positioned at the next critical juncture point where the coil needs to grow.

This discovery opens the hyperspacial door into the information networks that create the DNA in the first place. Once that door is opened, all hyperspacial information becomes intimately connected to our genetic foundations. When we include the fact that all information is connected, the possibility that therapy can influence our genetic roots becomes a high probability.

Any human "condition," thought to be the result of "inheritance" or "genetic factors," can now be tested. Can, for example, those who believe their sexual preferences are genetic in origin be influenced by a more holodynamic approach to life? During a six year period, between 1979 and 1984, 164 people who considered themselves "homosexual" became aware of Holodynamics. Most believed that their sexual preference had a "genetic" origin. While their sexual preference was not an "identified problem," it did become one of the issues that was addressed in their process of self-discovery. Of the 164 people, 160 chose to change their sexual preference. They changed from homosexual to heterosexual. Of the remaining four, one died and three chose to remain homosexual. Two of these were lesbians who chose to remain in relationship to each other. In a 12 year follow-up, they had switched partners, and one had given birth to a baby boy. The others had continued their heterosexual practice. If, as so many claim, homosexuality is a genetic condition, how was it that, in so many cases, the impact of their own self-discovery could have resulted in an apparent transformation induced by an "environmental" influence? Can therapy influence DNA?

The above incidences, from a scientific point of view, are an indication that either sexual preference is a conscious choice – in which case all arguments that homosexuality is genetic in origin are null and void - or it is DNA-sourced, and DNA can be changed by new information. Either way, it is worthy of serious research in the future.

In a conscious universe, where information weaves the web of life, therapy holds a public trust that permits exploration and change within all dimensions of reality. This trust takes the therapist beyond the limits of physical boundaries and into the whole dynamic of reality. Therapy can influence the DNA.

32. Unlimited energy: One key that unlocks the door to unlimited energy is enfolded within the mechanisms of consciousness. Take, for example, the mechanism of microtubules. "Microtubules" refers to the small (micro) tubes that were thought to make up the cytoskeleton of the body. They are like the threads that make up tissue of cells and organs, much like cotton threads make up the tissue in a shirt. Stuart Hameroff discovered that when the microtubules are anesthetized, there is no consciousness, no pain, neural growth, brain elasticity or other normal signs of consciousness (Hameroff). Further research indicates that microtubules are hollow inside, containing ionic pure water encased in valence-shifting dimer molecules, and are quantum in nature (Hameroff and Penrose). Others have picked up the research, birthing an entire new science, "the science of consciousness." (Refer to www.microtubules.com and to the University of Arizona, Science of Consciousness Department).

Microtubules are found in every living thing. They are considered primary mechanisms of consciousness and give off certain frequencies that create coherence in the body and communicate hyperspacially. For further references, see Woolf, Hameroff, Penrose and Gorgiev. The central role that microtubules play, as one of the mechanisms of consciousness, indicates they are crucial to consciousness and thus important in therapy. Refer to, *The Dance of Life: Transform your world NOW!* Woolf, 2005.

David Bohm's early works on "Science and the Implicate Order" first stimulated the work done with Holodynamic Therapy. The author applied the quantum premise to the internal environment within microtubules. His work in the Academy of Holodynamics (within the Academy of Natural Science of Russia) produced the theoretical foundations for a hyperspacial connection between the quantum potential fields in microtubules and other hyperspacial dimensions. This theoretical possibility helped understand numerous phenomena encountered in therapy (multiple personalities, delusions, illusions and some aspects of schizophrenia) that had no better explanation. Refer to *Holodynamics: How to Manage Your Personal Power*, 1990, and *The Dance of Life*, 2005.

Fine-grained and gross-grained screens cover the senses of the human body and create the holographic matrix controlling perception and information input. Karl Pribram identifies the reality of fine-grained and gross-grained screens that cover the human senses. The literature is replete with studies and examples of ongoing research on this subject. Mike Talbot and Ken Wilber have both produced excellent books on the holographic nature of the universe. Holograms are formed from wave references and information waves. Gross-grained screens let in the wave dynamics used for more contextual references in holograms. Fine-grained screens let in only smaller particles of information that can be used as specific content for holograms. These mechanisms indicate that senses are involved in the creation of the ongoing holographic matrix we experience as reality. Sensory input is translated into holographic form and transmitted to microtubules. The information is then stored as holodynes.

Frequencies used by holodynes to both send and receive information create quantum coherence in the body and affect multiple dimensions of consciousness. This assertion refers to work of S. Frohlech, who is recognized around the world for his contributions to superfluidity and superconductivity. In 1968, Frohlech predicted that biological systems would be found to exhibit quantum frequencies that create coherence in the body. His predictions have been confirmed and the implications are profound for psychologists. psychiatrists and for anyone involved in the field of therapy. As Roger Penrose has pointed out, "Microtubules are the perfect instruments for transmitting Frohlech frequencies."

Theoretically, holodynes are the perfect mechanisms for transmitting information within the Frohlech frequency ranges. This would explain how information is transmitted from hyperspace, into the microtubules, and then into the body. It also explains how information is received collectively and transmitted to "the swarm" in nature. This means that even the slightest thought or feeling is capable of being instantaneously transmitted to anyone, even to the collective. Can you imagine the impact of TV on people? Can you imagine what impact linear-dominated education is having upon individuals and society? Therapy cannot remain isolated from any aspect of consciousness.

Holodynes follow the same implicate order as do humans. This possibility was first proposed in 1968 during work with people who were seeking therapeutic intervention at the university who were assigned to Dr. Woolf (then working on his Ph.D. in Marriage and Family Therapy). As a developmental psychologist with a background in physics, Dr. Woolf proposed that information at all levels of organization followed a similar implicate order. For two years, his researchers gathered information on every known aspect of human consciousness and placed it within a developmental framework, seeking associations that would give indication of an implicate order of consciousness. Building upon the work of developmentalists, a comprehensive multidimensional topology was devised showing what was known at that time. During the therapy process, when this topology was utilized in the therapy process, people made extraordinary therapeutic progress in their personal growth. It was quite natural, then, to apply this framework to holodynes in the therapy process. This catapulted the therapy process into an entirely different dimension from which solutions emerged to a new level of therapeutic complexity. Holodynes responded to the same implicate order of growth. This became one of the foundation pillars of Holodynamic Therapy.

Microtubules work on quantum principles. Holodynes within the microtubules transmit Frohlech frequencies. These frequencies (in the range of 10 to the minus 33/sec) send information to the body. This information creates coherence among the organs and parts of the body. Holodynes can also create chaos. Disease is caused by incoherent holodynes that are creating chaos. Thus, theoretically, any disease can be "cured" by transforming the holodynes that are causing it. Therapists who understand this can be of great benefit in reversing the growing trends toward more and more complicated "dis-eases."

CHAPTER SEVEN

THERAPEUTIC SOLUTIONS

*T*HERAPEUTIC SOLUTIONS

34. Problems are caused by their solutions

Therapy honors each people's choice to have their problems and this enhances their ability to access solutions. Everyone has "problems. Some may seem worse than others but, in therapy, every problem is an opportunity to transform the problem into its solutions. [34]

Life can be viewed as a vacation. It is a vacation from our multidimensional, hyperspacial, quantum potential reality. We experience loss of self and the results are misery, deprivation, unhappiness and all our other limitations. We lose our Self in order to rediscover our Self. We lose our nature in order to rediscover our nature. We are born as less than our potential in order to choose to unfold our potential. It sometimes takes years, or even generations, for some people to create a really "good" problem. Therapy creates a growing environment, a morphogenic field, where solutions take form in the chaos of problems.

Therapy holds that problems are caused by their solutions. We create our problems so that we can "remember" solutions and rediscover our magnificent nature once again. Therapy discovers love when there is no reason to love. It discovers hidden truth where it is least likely to be found. It is a process that gives form to our solutions. Therapy honors each person and explores potential choices that lead to finding those solutions that have caused each of our problems.

35. Solutions within enfolded information systems

The therapist can reach beyond limited concepts of memory being "in the brain" and emotions "being the by-product of neurons," or "biochemistry." The therapist is willing to venture beyond the norms, into the quantum nature of dynamic information systems and to help people discover how to access these other dimensions of consciousness. [35] The fact that people are sometimes under the control of enfolded information systems does not make them "crazy." They may look crazy and act like they are "out of control," but the therapist understands hyperspacial and quantum information systems.

Therapists know about holodynes and microtubules and the processes by which they can transform what is not working. Seemingly erratic behavior has a message. All such behavior is driven by a potential that holds the keys to it own solution. Therapy can help find that message, discover how it all works, and help people decide the action that will make a difference in their lives. Even chaos has shape, color and a form. All holodynes originate somewhere, sometime and someplace. They organize and have intentions. They have a mode of operation. They can be accessed and transformed into their positive intent. Accessing these enfolded dimensions of information can unveil the solutions that are causing behavior that is counterproductive to well-being.

36. Solutions within symbiotic life forms

The human body contains millions of microscopic life forms. Some of these life forms have existed as a species for millions of years. Long before we humans came along, they had their own intelligence. We humans are symbiotic beings, part of a network of conscious life forms. Some of our holodynes come from these microscopic biological partners. They are quite capable of controlling our behavior via the Frohlech frequencies resonating from their holodynes. They make up part of our brain/neural systems, including our reptilian, mammalian and homeosapian brain stems, but they can also act independently. They have their own consciousness.

Their biological symbiosis with us is pre-programmed and coded to interact with us in our coherent field of consciousness. They can also get us out of balance and cause us problems such as rage, inappropriate sexual stimulation and depression. Those therapists who are aware of such primordial microscopic information systems, can teach us to communicate with these primitive life forms and, when necessary or helpful, the therapist can translate and help transform the holodynes upon which they operate so they do not damage their host. [36]

37. Solutions from inherited holodynes

Our microtubules contain inherited holodynes from a long line of ancestors.[37] These holodynes are transmitted through the microtubules in the sperm and egg. They are also reinforced in the intimate modeling of the family and culture as we grow up. This combination creates some of our most powerful holodynes. Some of these holodynes share many positive characteristics, helping us to survive and giving us a string of "instincts" and "inherited qualities" that help us be successful in life. We inherit entire cultural beliefs, family traditions, ancestral wisdom, character, ethical values and other life-supporting systems that are passed on from generation to generation. We also inherit misinformation.

Many of our myths, taboos and attitudes contain tendencies toward self-destruction and pathology. The therapist helps people distinguish between inherited holodynes and those that are current in people's lives. Therapy helps people redesign their genetic factors so that personal strengths can reinforce one's entire life potential.

38. Solutions from internal coherence processes

Legend has it that King Arthur was able to get the warring factions of his kingdom together by creating a round table process. The warring factions of the kingdom were able to meet on an equal basis and work out collaborative solutions to their problems. Therapy can provide a similar system of internal collaboration. Everyone has an internal community of holodynes that come from various sources. They were either inherited from ancestors, gleaned from experience, modeled from culture and society or come from parallel worlds. These holodynes are usually self-preserving and self-perpetuating. Their sometimes fierce independence can create internal conflict that shows up as dysfunctional behavior.[38] One moment the person may act one way and then, as another holodyne takes over, they can change behavior patterns so quickly it appears like "crazy making. Therapy provides the opportunity to create coherence. This can be done by creating an internal "place of peace," a "round table" for holodynes and even a "board of directors" that can "manage" the holodynes and establish balance. Thus therapy provides internal coherence.

39. Solutions from parallel worlds

We are living in multiple worlds where, from a quantum perspective, everything is connected, everything is conscious, and the past and future run in parallel to our present world.[39] Enfolded within the fabric of this matrix are dimensions of consciousness that are linked to all parallel worlds. Holodynes, for example, are able to connect hyperspacially with other worlds.

These parallel space-time continuums can have tremendous effect upon a person's life. When the influence of parallel worlds becomes self-organized in this time and space, the information "channeled" can cause splits in coherence, resulting in the appearance of multiple personalities and even schizophrenia. Therapy can help access and understand these parallel worlds. It can create a therapeutic environment for the transformation and healing of the whole dynamic.

Usually, the person sensitized to information from parallel dimensions serves as a "messenger." This person may also become a potential "facilitator" of well-being, not only in this world, but in parallel worlds as well. Therapy utilizes parallel worlds because the solution to any problem is found within the source of the problem. Therapy facilitates solutions from parallel worlds.

40. Solutions from our collective covenant

Information, no matter what its source, is passed on from generation to generation. Family beliefs, for example, are both inherited and modeled for us so we understand that family holodynes are one of the main causes of human behavior. Therapy identifies holodynes that are causing problems and facilitates transforming of holodynes by treating the whole family. Our experiences with family members are part of the family "covenant." [40] In some dimension of consciousness, each family member has agreed to create their experiences and also their "problems." Usually this "mutual creation" indicates a "collective covenant."

Family members have, in some dimension, agreed to what transpires so that they can then manifest the solutions together. In therapy, the process of family therapy is natural. Sometimes all therapy means is just creating space for solutions to happen. Life is self-organizing. Sometimes all that solutions need is an environment in which to grow. Everything is connected. This is the therapy environment. It is one that allows the psychological space to treat the whole person and the whole family no matter where the holodynes originate. The same is true for any relationship, group, or those who share a collective consciousness. Life is managed by covenants - hyperspacial, pre-computed, agreements. Therapy provides a morphogenic field for solutions that reflect coherence with collective covenants. Solutions are found in the nature of the collective covenants.

41. Solutions and the environment for change

Consciousness emerges through its environment. While the consciousness of each person emerges through specific stages of development, it cannot be isolated from its intimate environment. If one does not understand the stages of development for well-being or its connection to the implicate order of its environment, the possibilities of doing therapy are limited to a type of Russian roulette. Therapy is not a game of Russian roulette.

Therapy is an alignment process wherein one's consciousness aligns with the implicate order of the quantum field. [41] Since that field is multidimensional, it includes holodynes, information from hyperspacial parallel worlds, including the past, present and future - and it includes family and cultural influences, as well as self-created holodynes. Each of these dimensions must, potentially, be included. Each contains a potential menu of options that set the therapeutic stage for change. Solutions emerge from an environment for change.

42. Solutions beyond the emotional model

There are no solutions to anything when one is confined to "feelings." The "heart" is not sufficient, in and of itself, to handle life. [42] "E-motions" or "energy in motion" does not provide a model capable of containing reality. Wave dynamics are not enough and they can never be enough. Quantum physics has contributed a great deal to our understanding of the wave dynamics of reality. These contributions have led to major new technological developments and to new insights into the nature of consciousness.

Quantum dynamics within the body explain much about non-linear aspects of consciousness, including emotions, feelings and values. Quantum thinking, however, cannot contain reality anymore than emotions can offer solutions to our problems. Therapy reaches beyond emotions to embrace presence in a holodynamic world.

43. Solutions beyond the rational model

There are no solutions to anything when one is confined to "thinking." The "head" is not sufficient, in and of itself, to handle life. The rational mind does not provide a model capable of containing reality. Particle dynamics are not enough and they can never be enough. Classical physics has contributed a great deal to our understanding of the particle dynamics of reality. These contributions have helped free humankind from many of the limiting aspects of the past. Linear science has established the productivity of the Industrial Age and formed the basis for our current education, social, government and financial world. The price society pays is high. The result has been a continuing expansion of prison populations, mental illness, drug and alcohol abuse, continual chaos, and management by crisis, to mention a few. Half the children drop out of school before graduating from high school.

Linear thinking cannot contain reality any more than thoughts can offer solutions to our problems. Therapy reaches beyond linear, rational thinking to embrace presence, that state of being fully conscious in a holodynamic world. [43]

44. Solutions from transformation of the past

The idea that therapy is just a lot of "talk, talk, talk" is no longer acceptable. Talk therapy is not the "best deal" in town. To remember an event, to tell a story, or to recall the past only makes sense when it makes it possible to *"Re-live"* the past. Reliving *transforms* the past. While many people want to deal with the past and love to "tell their stories," stories are only holodynes speaking out. Holodynes are self-preserving and self-perpetuating. They will, through their stories, only reinforce what has happened in the past in the hope of assuring a similar future. People understand that to just keep on telling old stories only reinforces the holodynes that hold the problem in place.

Therapy takes place once people grasp the possibility that *the past is running parallel to the present.[44]* They can then can re-enter the past at their fullest potential, access its information, and transform it. Accompanied by their Full Potential Self, people can access any information necessary for completing such transformations. They can change their old ways of looking at events, "Re-live" experiences looking through the eyes of the Full Potential Self and understand more completely what each experience was all about.

They can learn what covenants were involved, learn the lessons to be learned and potentialize those experiences, not just talk about it. They can re-experience stored memories from a new state of being that creates a new point of view. This transformation produces extraordinary results. Reliving the past in a conscious universe is part of what makes this a "plan-it."

45. Solutions from the future

Therapy also provides the opportunity to "pre-live" events. Parallel worlds exist beyond time. Any "beyond time" dimension includes worlds of the future. When people access information fields from the future, they can also integrate this information into the present. This process requires the correlation of the Full Potential Self and a state of being universal. From a quantum perspective, the past, present, and future are all running in parallel. People see it in the movies and hear it in speeches. [45]

The old theories have not worked that well and people want to understand these new ones. They want the future now - especially that future that resolves their troubles. Many are trying to apply "Pre-live" processes into their lives. At best, it's a "hit-and-miss" effort. Therapy, however, provides the opportunity to systematically discover how "beyond time" dimensions can apply to creating well-being. "Pre-living" is an opportunity to explore possibilities that occur in hyperspace as part of the network of consciousness that contains the menu of options for the future. Therapy can help gain access to this information through the "Pre-live" process. All solutions to our daily problems can be found in the future.

46. Solutions as integration

Therapy integrates every dimension of consciousness into one's state of consciousness. Creating an internal "Place of Peace" and accessing one's Full Potential Self creates coherence, changes our view and promotes genuine presence. The transformation of holodynes and the "Re-live" and "Pre-live" processes are examples of how we can integrate the past and the future into the present. [46]

Processes like this form the infrastructure of mental well-being. People know. They sense it and they want it. They want therapists who help integrate solutions. Therapy can help create a "Place of Peace" in a person's mind; serve as a refuge from the stress and chaos of daily lives; "anchor" consciousness; stimulate; and communicate with the Full Potential Self and with transformed holodynes. Therapy can help organize a "Round Table" where holodynes can meet, negotiate and come to resolution about conflicts in a person's internal world. This internal guidance system can give an indication of actions that people can best take in their daily living. In other words, therapy provides specific, workable, solution processes that people can take home and use every day.

FOOTNOTES - CHAPTER SEVEN

33. Personal and collective potential: One of the basic tenants of quantum physics is that every set of circumstances is driven by potential (Bohm et al, 1987). Personal and collective consciousnesses (like any other "set of circumstances") are "driven by potential." (Woolf, 1990 and 2005).

34. Problems caused by their solutions: What people label as a "problem" can also be identified as "a given set of circumstances" (refer to footnote 33). Thus, each "problem" is "driven by potential." Over the past few decades, the identification of certain problems and their "potential solutions" has led to the irrevocable conclusion that, not only are problems "driven" by "potential," but they are "driven by their "potential solution. Solutions found by using a holodynamic approach include overcoming drug abuse (in six American cities), solving mental illness (over 80% of a state mental hospital population returned to community life); reform of maximum prisoners (until we were asked to stop); street gangs (600 gang members back to academic standards); major corporate changes (Boeing, Toyota, Bank of America); helping to end the Cold War (10 year effort – see Woolf, 2005); and successfully dealing with terrorists in the Middle East (see "Bombs in the Olive Garden" www.holodynamics.com/articles and Woolf, 2005).

35. Enfolded Information Systems: Thousands of books and articles have been written about enfolded information systems. Beginning with the findings of Freud, Jung, Adler and a host of others, entire schools of thought have arisen regarding this subject. These new pioneer sciences have shed new light on enfolded information systems that not only make for better understanding, but also better therapy. From developmental psychology, we glean that there are six main categories of enfolded within (Woolf, 1990). From physics and mathematics, we learn of at least 10 possible dimensions enfolded within our sense of reality. See footnotes 1-14 for more details. The book, *The Dance of Life* and the five Manuals that expand upon the text, cover in some detail enfolded information systems (Woolf, 2005).

36. Symbiotic life forms: One of the least understood symbiotic life forms is bacteria. Yet bacteria are responsible for life on earth. According to the record in the rocks, life began on earth in the form of prokaryotic bacteria. The prokaryocytes first showed up on earth about 5 billion years ago. For about 3.5 billion years they were the only life form evident. They were simple cells without vertebra or organs but they could divide and communicate, not the way we communicate, but through what appears to be sexual exchange. They "injected" information into each other. Then, about 1.5 billion years ago, eukaryotic bacteria appeared. The Eukaryotes are far more complex. In fact, they were so sophisticated that humans have not been able to duplicate what they can do. The Eukaryotes are able to take sunlight and change it into complex carbohydrates in a process called "photosynthesis." They can also conduct more than 360 complex chemical procedures within the walls of the cell. And one of these chemical procedures could destroy the cell.

These so called "primitive bacteria" are responsible for creating a balanced atmosphere that contains about 20% oxygen. They have arranged for the emergence of all plant and animal life on earth. They have created the ozone level, maintain constant temperature, oxygen and salt content in the ocean, and are part of every life form on the planet. They also are involved in symbiotic relationship with the human body.

Scientists have attempted to duplicate photosynthesis. Only one attempt has produced any results. It is a large laboratory that has many complex machines and produces approximately one gram of sugar per day. The tree outside the window of the lab produces five pounds a day. Humans have intelligence but we are not alone in this regard. Bacteria have also exhibited profound intelligence. We can see their history of accomplishments in the rocks. What makes us think they are not still active within the consciousness of the planet and within our own conscious systems? They are and with little training, people can access these incredible symbiotic life forms and gain information from them.

Bacteria are not the only symbiotic life forms that exist within the human body. See *Lives of a Cell: Notes of a Biology Watcher* by Lewis Thomas, who points out that millions of symbiotic entities dwell within us. He writes:

> "We are not made up, as we had always supposed, of successively enriched packets of our own parts. We are shared, rented, occupied. At the interior of our cells, driving them, providing the oxidative energy that sends us out for the improvement of each shining day, are the mitochondria, and in a strict sense, they are not ours. They turn out to be little separate creatures, the colonial posterity of migrant prokaryocytes, probably primitive bacteria that swam into ancestral precursors of our eukaryotic cells and stayed there. Ever since, they have maintained themselves and their ways, replicating in their own fashion, privately, with their own DNA and RNA quite different from ours. They are as much symbionts as the rhizobial bacteria in the roots of beans. Without them, we would not move a muscle, drum a finger, or think a thought ..."

Why should the practice of therapy be considered anything less that "sensitive" to the symbiotic life forms within us? Add to this immense reservoir of influence, the other dimensions of consciousness and therapy becomes a constant conversation with multiple symbiotic life forms. (Woolf, 2005).

37. Inherited holodynes: Using holographics, it is evident that memory is stored as holodynes within the microtubules (Woolf, 1990). Electron microscopes show clearly that both the sperm and the egg contain microtubules (see *National Geographic*, Aug. 1998). In addition, using vortex sciences and spinner technologies, it is evident that information is available from hyperspace, outside of the confines of time. Thus information can be transmitted from one generation to the next. Examination of belief systems, split-twin studies and genealogical records give ample evidence to show that information is passed on from one generation to the next (Woolf, 2005). Because of the quantum nature of memory storage within the microtubules, it is possible that the entire history of humanity could be inherited.

38. Internal coherence: There are numerous references to studies concerning quantum coherence in the microtubules, brain and body. In Finland, Matti Pitkanan, at the University of Finland's Department of Theoretical Physics, has suggested that quantum coherence "in the brain" is influenced by Bose Einstein condensates. (See www.physics.helsinki.fi/~matpitka/tubules.html - 73k).

From Stanford University, Mark Shwartz (contact mshwartz@stanford.edu) reports observing microtubules involved in almost every aspect of plant life, including "treadmilling" within the growth process of cells. So much information is now available on the role of microtubules in creating internal coherence that one can find more than 90,000 references on the Internet (see www.microtubules.com). These articles deal with the biological, chemical, physics and mathematics of consciousness. Damion Brunner, from the University of Zurich, Switzerland, reports on postdoctoral research at the Imperial Cancer Research Fund in London, UK, the following:

"During the development of a multicellular organism, cells must differentiate into specific cell types. Ultimately, every cell needs to end up in the right position and with a particular shape. In general, cellular morphology is dependent on a high degree of polarization. This is achieved by arranging the cytoskeleton of cells, mainly actin and cytoplasmic microtubules, in an appropriate way to allow the polar distribution of organelles and cellular factors." (Refer to "Cellular morphogenesis and microtubule guidance" at fusionanomaly.net/microtubules.html).

In other words, coherence among cells depends upon microtubules. Since coherence in life is intimately connected to microtubules, therapy that is concerned with internal coherence would do well to focus on the microtubules, in order to better understand internal coherence. As pointed out earlier in this writing, everything is conscious and its coherence is part of its nature. It is just a lot more complex than any prior generation could conceive. A topology of Holodynamics was created in order to help understand its complexity. (Woolf, 1990).

39. Parallel worlds: Gone are the days when people who communicate with parallel worlds are thought of as "mentally ill." The actual existence of parallel worlds has put the matter straight. Fred Alan Wolf, a renowned quantum physicist writes:

> "The parallel universes hypothesis enriches the field of psychology. For example, it may help us to understand major disorders now appearing rampant in our societies, such as multiple personalities and schizophrenia." (Wolf, Fred A., "Parallel Universes" 1995).

A number of scientists have gone into considerable detail in exploring parallel worlds. Not only does the theory better explain a number of observable data, but, in psychology, the existence of parallel worlds explains that phenomenon of consciousness that cannot be explained any other way (Woolf, 2005).

40. The collective covenant: See footnotes 1-8 above. The "collective covenant" refers to a dimension of consciousness in which all consciousness is connected. Something similar to the "grand unified theory" or "M-theory" (Hawking, 2001), the "covenant" indicates that everything people do, think or feel in space-time is connected. This dimension of the covenant is sometimes referred to as the "superposition" of consciousness. (Woolf, 2005). The superposition dimension exists beyond space-time. Thus, any information from one generation is available in any other generation. All that is required is overcoming the "time" barrier. Humans have the innate ability to overcome the time barrier and travel in time (see footnotes 1, 2, 3 and 23).

41. Consciousness and the environment: Environment refers to those influences, both internal and external, that affect consciousness. Literally, "environment" refers not only to physical, social and cultural influences, but also to multidimensional fields of consciousness. Each person's thoughts and feelings, body, mind and spirit, so to speak, are contained within a network of holographic information systems that are connected to every other system – including hyperspace. All are part of nature. We are interwoven in a magnificent matrix of consciousness.

42. Therapy beyond the emotional model: Quantum physics allowed scientists to deal with "wave" dimensions of reality from a series of "probabilities" and "abstracts. This was a significant move beyond the linear, particalized thinking of the few hundred years before the quantum age. And, in spite of the amazing progress the world has made using quantum physics, the science of quantum physics has no answers to some of the most profound challenges on the planet. Why? Because wave dynamics cannot contain all of reality. Emotions can be defined in "wave" terms but they cannot be made responsible for the network of consciousness in which they are interwoven. Therapy works when it is embracive, all inclusive and sensitive to the holodynamic of consciousness (Woolf, 2005).

43. Therapy beyond the rational model: Evident in the patterns of emerging life are strong indications that linear thinking cannot contain reality. There are just too many things that cannot be analyzed, broken into parts, placed in neat little boxes and measured according to classical physics. Our traditional approach, using Newtonian thinking, has led to serious limitations in every branch of society including schools, churches, correctional facilities, economics, government and therapy. Therapy works when the process moves beyond linear models because, by its nature, therapy embraces even those dimensions of reality that are beyond the scope of linear thinking (Woolf, 2005).

44. Transforming the past: Over the past century, our view of reality has been infused with new concepts that have brought forth an explosion of new technology and an entirely new way to experience life. Einstein's theory of general relativity, for example, places one's experience of reality dependant upon one's position. This general relativity approach showed space and time as interwoven, dynamic and anything but linear. Space and time are "bent" by transdimensional gravitational influences. Space-time has curved dimensions that bend light, curve time and place the past the future into a space-time "knot," allowing consciousness to access the past and the future (Hawking, 2001; Wolf, 1995).

45. "Preliving" the future: While it may be difficult for some people to imagine, according to the best evidence available, the future is running in parallel with the present. We can access this dimension and "pre-live" it. See footnote 44.

46. Integration: Integration refers to the process of incorporating the parts into a whole. In a multidimensional world, the process of integration incorporates all dimensions within one's state of conscious being (see footnotes 1-95). The process of integration includes accessing and aligning with hyperspace, including one's Full Potential Self and parallel dimensions of consciousness. Integration also requires accessing and aligning (often transforming) one's holodynes, micro biotic life forms (including cells and organs of the body), relationships and systems including environmental systems. Since we are nested within one whole dynamic information matrix, integration is considered a major objective of therapy. One process for integration is the "round table" process. Others include Place of Peace, daily planning, Tracking, Re-living, Pre-living and potentializing. For details refer to *The Dance of Life*, Woolf, 2005 and the manuals, 2005-6.

CHAPTER EIGHT

THERAPY AND THE OPEN MARKET

*T*HERAPY AND THE OPEN MARKET

47. Therapy is a "product" on the open market

Therapy is a "product" on the open market, a service for hire, and our customers are looking for the best deal possible. Therapy is no longer cloaked under an aura of mystery because there is nothing mysterious about therapy. The doors of different types of therapy are open and people are the consumers. Part of therapy is to provide the public with accurate information about what they are paying for ahead of time.[47] This knowledge is part of the public domain, which is available on the Internet and detailed enough so that people can review it before they apply for services. Therapists are in the business of consulting with people about their personal lives and helping them find solutions to their problems. The public has the right to be choosey about buying therapy services and to obtain the best product available at the best price possible.

48. Therapy is efficient and effective

Therapy is not about the therapist. Listening for hours while a therapist proliferates about their experiences, theories, "plans" or "strategies" is a waste of time. Therapy provides an environment of genuine concern with a therapist who cares enough to focus on the customer in a way that stimulates therapeutic movement. If there is no movement, it may be that therapy is not happening. Therapy provides an efficient and effective process by which people can align with their potential, identify their holodynes, transform what is necessary, apply the new information in life and gain the internal coherence necessary for psychological well-being, even if it takes them into parallel worlds. Therapy can be short term, follow the implicate order, and still be effective. It's not about the therapist; it's about the client.[48]

FOOTNOTES - CHAPTER EIGHT

47. The "best deal possible": One of the characteristics of an open market. People "shop," in an open market to purchase goods of the highest quality in exchange for the least possible money.

48. Efficiency: Refers to the ability to produce the desired effect. Therapy practices are noted for their lack of efficiency in the past, but the new information allows therapy to become more efficient and more effective. Part of this improvement is due to the fact that information systems self-organize. Some of the most advanced work on self-organizing information systems has come from work done with quantum computers (see Woolf and Blue, 2001). Since the intention of the therapy process is usually to aid in the self-organization of information, the laws of self-organizing information systems can now be applied to the therapy process.

CHAPTER NINE

WHO IS THE THERAPIST?

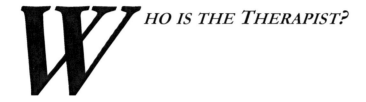

WHO IS THE THERAPIST?

49. Therapists are "present"

Therapists are most effective when the therapist is "present. This means therapists are aligned with their own Full Potential Self.[49] Therapists do their homework. They have worked on their own relationships with their own potential and come into the therapy session ready to help people align with their own Full Potential Self. Therapists have matured their own holo-dynes and created their own internal system of coherence. They are balanced and able to maintain a state of psychological well-being.

Therapists cannot model what they have not achieved in their personal lives. Personal presence creates comfortable in the presence of another. It is in this "state of being present" that people resolve their problems. The therapist is present.

50. The therapist is transparent

Whether they want to admit it or not, therapists are transparent.[50] The public can see right through into their problems and limitations. Everyone has problems. When we are willing to admit it rather than hide it, we have begun the therapy process. People want a friend and consultant, one who resonates with information that is consistent with what is being said. Therapists cannot afford the luxury of being afraid of their own limitations, their personal potential, or the joys of being. The therapist is transparent.

51. The therapist is both "in" and "out" of the therapy process

The therapist is not just an observer. In a quantum world, there is no such thing as an "objective" observer. The therapist is both "in" and "out" of the therapy process at the same time.[51] Therapists recognize that being "in" the process of therapy increases their comprehension of the experience and facilitates therapeutic movement. At the same time, the therapist does not want to be caught up in the same event horizons as the client. Being "out" of the problem permits new information to be brought into the process. In this way, the therapist enters the state of being in which distinctions can be made and choice become available in his own life as well as in the life, of others.

52. The Therapist is accountable

Any professional sales representative understands that a conversation takes place eye-to-eye, face-to-face, and human-to-human. Public relations cannot take place from an answering machine where one person has to leave a message. Therapy is not about an e-mail relationship where people e-mail the therapist a message and then read his or her response. Maybe, sometimes, it's necessary, but there are some pre-conditions. Therapy is about being able to sense the real human being - the friend, the warmth and the supportive being who is the therapist. Therapy is about the *being of togetherness* that bonds people and creates a morphogenetic field for growth. It is a multidimensional covenant.[52]

Therapy is about touching souls, bonding and knowing the therapist is safe – one of the "count-on-ables." Then, in person, on the phone, on the answer phone, or by e-mail, it doesn't matter, because people know each other personally. They know the "us" of the relationship and are safe in that knowledge and can create therapy.

53. Therapists and participants are part of the same field

Therapist can take notes from the holographic paradigm - "what is known to the part is known to the whole and what is known to the whole is known to each part." Everything in the universe is conscious of the information from which it is made because it is inclusive not exclusive in nature.[53] The old idea that humans have the "highest" or "best developed" or "most evolved" form of consciousness is false. Likewise, the idea that a therapist knows more than the participant, is separate, or isolated, is likewise false. It flies in the face of holographic reality, and anything that flies in the face of reality is counter-therapeutic.

54. The therapist "is" the therapy

Therapy takes place when hyperspacial quantum computing pre-empts conscious thought. Such computing takes place in a dynamic quantum field. That is, the field itself is conscious, ever-changing, and still maintaining an implicate order. This field is reflected by the therapist.[54]

Gone are the days when a therapist could sit on a couch and "think" the client through a linear process of change. Any therapist who sits back on a couch, without the eye-to-eye communication with a person, hidden from personal involvement, fearful of transference and defending against counter-transference, is not being a therapist. A therapist is therapeutic when he or she "becomes" the therapy process when he or she gets out of the linear mind and emotional constrictions and enters the holodynamic state of being in touch with reality.

The process of therapy cannot be contained within the mind of the analyst or within the heart of a rescuer. The information field, the process of therapy and the therapist are one whole dynamic. Therapists cannot remain aloof from the power of their own personal impact upon therapy. The therapist must "become" the process. This can only be accomplished from a holodynamic state of being. Consciousness is holodynamic, and the therapist "is" the therapy.

FOOTNOTES - CHAPTER NINE

49. Presence: Alignment with one's hyperspacial counterpart. Such alignment allows all dimensions of reality to be manifest in a person's current consciousness. Presence is the most primary of all human conditions. Likewise, presence is the most primary of all therapy goals. It is the key to psychological well-being (Woolf, 2005).

50. Transparency: The ability to remain clear or coherent and to be experienced by others from that state of being. The therapist expects transparency from those asking for therapy and they expect it from the therapist. Transparency is a two-way street. Integrity requires it. (Woolf, 2005).

51. The "in" and "out" of therapy: Refers to quantum qualities of information systems that run in parallel. (See Woolf & Blue, 2002).

52. The "Count-on-ables": One of the expressions given to a reliable therapist.

53. The Holographic Information Field: See Hawking, (2001); Wilber, (1982); Woolf, 2005.

54. The therapist "is" the therapy: Refers to the "state of being" that reflects the coherence of one's title (in this case, "therapist") with one's holodynamic condition.

CHAPTER TEN

THERAPY AND TECHNOLOGY

*T*HERAPY AND *T*ECHNOLOGY

55. Therapy tools include the Internet

Some of the modern technological tools available to the therapist are things like the telephone, video conferencing, mail, e-mail or the Internet. The prerequisite for therapy using these tools is *presence*. Therapy resonates with hyperspacial presence.[55] Such resonation frequencies are carried via the microtubules and are carried, in part, by voice, during the therapy process in the therapy office when people are speaking to each other. But such frequencies are also quantum in nature. They can also be transmitted over phone or via video conferencing. They also prove effective when transmitted through written words, as in a letter, or by e-mail. Information is conveyed via Frohlech frequencies, hyperspacially, beyond time and space. Therapy information can be part of a collective or highly individualized consciousness. As long as it reflects presence, it is therapy. The Internet can be a therapeutic tool as long as it reflects presence.

56. There are no hidden agendas in therapy

Therapy is not the imposition of external values or prescriptions upon individuals. It is not organized to bring a person into conformity with the rules of society. It is not to take away from a person's own power. Rather, it is to facilitate the person's own resources to accomplish their goals.[56]

Within the information field of the Full Potential Self is everything needed to overcome a person's challenges and make a maximum contribution to society and to life. Therapy is about honoring people, being honest and sharing the adventure. Anything less is not therapeutic. There is no external technology that can create therapy. There can be no hidden agendas in therapy.

57. People-to-people versus doctor-to-patient

People have figured out that they can get more reliable information from their people networks than they can from professional pill-pushers or service vendors. An informed public understands the profit motive and professional corporate rhetoric about the added value of their commoditized products. They know more about the value of services or medications than the drug companies, corporations or professionals who distribute their own products. The therapist cannot serve two masters.[57]

As "one of the people," the therapists must stand on the "people side" of the fence, translating the corporate rhetoric and adapting all information for the benefit of the people in therapy. Standing together, everyone can survive and thrive in a field of psychological health.

FOOTNOTES - CHAPTER TEN

55. The Internet: See Levine et al., 2001, that outlines some of the principles of doing business in a world where the Internet is available (see also footnotes 56 and 57).

56. Hidden Agendas: One of the fundamental discoveries of quantum physics is that everything, in some dimension of reality, is connected (Bohm, Hawking, Woolf, 2005). In a quantum world, there can be no secrets and there is no separation. It is the public trust that anyone who accepts the mantle of "therapist" will act according to the fundamental discoveries of science in the application of the practice of therapy.

57. People-to-people: Information theory suggests: "Relationship is everything" (Kelly). While this may seem like an overstatement, there is sufficient research to show that the statement has considerable merit, especially when considered from certain dimensions of reality where relationships have their "being." Consider the collective or swarm intelligence. Flocks of birds, swarms of bees or termites, armies of ants, schools of fish and even an individual cell cannot exist without relationships. Likewise, from a holographic view, as another example, anything that exists has a "counterpart" in hyperspace. Without this "relationship" nothing in our space-time continuum would exist. Therapy, from the holodynamic dimensions, is people-to-people or it does not exist (Woolf, 2005).

Therapy and Technology

CHAPTER ELEVEN

THERAPY AND THE "COMPANY"

*T*HERAPY AND THE *"C*OMPANY*"*

58. Pharmaceutical companies and professional therapists are also people

The public understands the difference between the metaphysical "company," or "professional," and "the person." People share similar experiences and challenges. Just because a therapist has received a degree from an educational institution or works for a pharmacy company that produces drugs does not mean the therapist is not a person. Any person can have a mental health problem. The concept of "company" or "professional" cannot stand between people in the therapy process. The company and the professional are interested in "markets" and "profits" while the people are interested in people. The therapist can tell the difference and puts people on the top of the priority list.[58]

59. The company cannot prescribe therapy

Neither insurance companies, pharmacies, medical associations, nor professionals who have been trained to script their sales rhetoric, can prescribe therapy. The company speaks a different language and has a different motive. It remains aloof, distant from people and their feedback.[59]

This distancing stance creates a breakdown in communication. The corporate voice is hollow and flat – literally, "inhuman. It must come down off the mountain, stop playing God, and get real, people to people. Until it does that, it cannot prescribe therapy because it does not know its own people - let alone a total stranger. The company cannot prescribe therapy.

60. Company diagnostic tools don't work

Therapy focuses on treatment and success procedures, not just on diagnosis of the problems. Diagnosis tends to put people in boxes. It encourages everyone to treat people like some form of specimen. Therapy does not put people in cages. They will not stay caged up.

They will resist with everything they have — even self-destruction — before they will be denied their human nature. This same quality is reflected throughout nature. The condition of the potential photon, before it becomes a physical photon, takes on meaning only after it takes on form and is potentialized.

Likewise, the focus of therapy provides meaning when it is directed toward potential solutions that are causing the problems. Therapy is the act of potentializing the problem. Problems are presented in order to discover potential solutions. The corporate diagnostic process is counterproductive to the therapy process. The therapy service industry must move beyond diagnostic thinking because it does not work. It's a sham. Anyone can fit into any of those categories. Who are we trying to kid? Company dialogues don't work. There is another way.[60]

61. Presence subverts hierarchies

Therapy does not require pyramids of power, authority structures, or distancing between the therapist and those who participate in the therapy process. In fact, presence is open, honest, genuine personal communication. Hierarchies cannot survive in such an atmosphere. It is counterproductive to therapy to think of people in therapy as some form of sub-species, to be studied, experimented with and then discarded while the therapist goes to lunch.[61]

Have lunch together. People are all, in one sense, marooned on this little lifeboat called the "plan-it." "Being" together can help potentialize our problems. Presence always subverts hierarchies.

62. Therapy cannot depend upon drugs

People, like everything else, can be blocked in the emergence of their consciousness. Therapy proceeds when the blocks are identified and transformed according to their own implicate order. Therapy cannot depend upon drugs alone to do the job. Drugs have not been known to "cure" anything. At best, they stimulate the body's natural immune system to do its job and get on with the process. Therapy invites an internal conversation. It is an exchange of information. That is the heart of the therapy process and it cannot depend on drugs.[62]

63. People are insulated against advertising

People can tell when others are handing them "the party line." The best advice is: "Just forget it." It does not matter if one is giving a speech, passing out business cards, or holding some special seminar on some special topic. People can tell when anyone is advertising. When a therapist has to market himself, he is already "gone" and so are the people. The conscious universe has free will and since therapy is the exercise of free will, therapy includes all conscious forms involved in choice. Choice exists at every level of reality. The biosphere maintains itself on the planet. Photons choose the form they take according to the choices they are given (particle or wave).[63]

Microscopic organisms that make up the body, exhibit the ability to choose their participation in bodily functions. Microtubules choose the elements that are needed in the body and pass them on. They place minerals and proteins exactly where they are needed. Every atom, protein string, living cell, organ of the body, person, group, or nation has choice. Choice "is." Holodynes have choice. Therapy provides the experience of accessing, communicating, negotiating, and transforming information systems according to their own choice so as to align with the fullest possible potential of the therapy experience. The universe supports life by its own free will. The universe supports therapy (as long as it really is therapy). The universe supports the therapist and the therapist does not advertise. The therapist communicates.

64. Therapy cannot be conducted from an ivory tower

When a therapist is afraid of his own presence — hiding behind all those books and degrees up on the office walls — and when he must distance himself — fortified by the corporate or professional mentality, or by past successes — he cannot have a relationship with people who come for therapy. Declaring oneself a "success" is not "being" successful. Marketing oneself puts one in the same frame as marketeers. Marketeers are afraid of the public eye. They do not want anyone to know what is really going on inside the company. People do not want to be fed marketing "hype" because they become suspicious and cannot go on together if there is no trust in each other. Therapists tell it like it is. Presence is a great gift.[64]

65. There are no secrets

We live in an Information Age. There are "chat rooms" and Internet networks that can give people almost unlimited information about their symptoms and problems. This information moves the public far beyond what was possible in the past days of the closed doors of mental hospitals. People are informed about what is known about their condition and what can be done about it. They can converse with others who have had similar conditions and learn what works and what doesn't work. They don't want to be "sold" on something that does not work. They are a much more aware public. There are no secrets.[65]

FOOTNOTES - CHAPTER ELEVEN

58. The company: Once one understands the collective nature of consciousness, "the company" is viewed as a distinct, self-organizing, information system with its own consciousness. It is a collective, held in place by those who service it as personnel. This collective has its own "being. This is referred to as "The Being Of System's Synergy" ("BOSS").

In most cases, the BOSS has its own agenda, its own interests and its own culture that has little, if anything, to do with the individuals that make up its constituates. In fact, the BOSS may be so self-centered that it overrules those who work for the company. It was this very dynamic that led to the formation of counter-systems, like unions, secretarial pools, and the like.

The key to finding solutions to the dominance of a self-serving BOSS rests in the fact that everything has a built-in order of growth (see footnote 15). Cultivating a growing corporate culture provides a dynamic field in which individual consciousness and the collective consciousness, can be interwoven into a network of win-win processes (Woolf, 2005). When the BOSS remains ineffective, the entire system suffers.

59. Prescriptions: While there appears to be limited value to some prescribed medications, most prescriptions are motivated by money. Pharmaceutical firms have formed a vice-like global cartel controlled by private and public agencies over the medical well-being of society. The public, however, is becoming informed and, with the advent of new technology, such as the Internet, the "company" can no longer prescribe drugs to treat symptoms. See Levine, Woolf, 2005 for more details.

60. Company diagnostic tools: While this point may be self-evident to those who have their computers invaded with "spam," their mail-boxes overloaded with junk mail and even their telephone lines infested with corporate sales representatives, there is a basis for public resistance. The company "mind" is "distanced" from the individual. See Woolf, *The Dance of Life* 2005, *Manual IV and Manual V*, 2006.

61. Hierarchies: See Woolf, *The Dance of Life,* 2005, for a summary of projects that demonstrate this point.

62. Drugs: The promise of, or hope for, an "easy fix" for psychological health has not materialized. There are no effective medications for most types of mental illness. What the pharmaceutical firms have offered is mostly symptomatic treatments. The best that we can do is to stimulate the body's natural immune system to take over the job. The sad news is that every professional therapist knows it.

63. Advertising: See Levine. In the world of business, anyone expecting to obtain a part of the market must be aware of the potential for updraft or downdraft effects.

64. The Ivory Tower: A distancing process by which one person, because of position or status, or some other rational, assumes superiority to another. When this position is taken by a therapist, therapy ends. See footnotes 1-14.

65. Secrets: To keep information exclusive of others is a common practice but such a practice is always based upon a limited consciousness (see Woolf, 1990, 2005). Information is power. From a linear perspective, this statement means something like, "I must keep information secret in order to maintain power." From a wave perspective secrets are only a passing fancy. But from a holodynamic view, there are no secrets. In some dimension, everything is connected. This is a basic finding of quantum physics (Bohm). It is also a basic premise of the science of consciousness (Penrose, Pribram, Gorgiev, and Woolf).

CHAPTER TWELVE

WHAT IS THERAPY?

WHAT IS THERAPY?

66. Therapy is a covenant

The therapist is chosen because somewhere, sometime, in some dimension, each person has made a covenant to do therapy with the therapist. A covenant is an agreement. Hyperspacial entanglements and their constant information exchange in the quantum field suggest that physical reality exists by agreement among all "qubits" of information spinner networks in hyperspace. Similarly, life is able to sustain its collaboration because all life forms are connected by a free will, conscious "covenant."

It is this hyperspacial intelligent network that sustains a living biosphere.[66] It also allows everything to experience its uniqueness. Each experience we undergo in life is part of this covenant. People, societies, animals, plants, insects and elements all live under the covenant. From the superposition of quantum computing, consciousness of the Full Potential Self pre-empts personal consciousness and, even though we may not recognize it, the Full Potential Self has made the covenant.

Therapy facilitates the experience of coming into conscious understanding of the covenant and discovers why each experience is chosen. Therapy helps find the solution that drives every problem. It unveils the meaning of life's struggles — its pain, sorrow and challenges. We create a life and experience its challenges in order to find solutions. We appear ignorant in order to rediscover our wisdom. We lose our own identities in order to find ourselves. Life is a "vacation" from our real nature and we all agreed to take this vacation. Sometimes we want to remember and visit home again. Therapy is a part of this covenant. It is an invitation to remember the covenant. Therapy is a covenant.

67. Therapy is a dynamic exchange of information

The universe is made of information *in motion*. The universe is NOT made of little solid atoms, and people are not "cases." Mass and matter are formed from information "spinners" emerging from hyperspace. The ancient division between body, mind and spirit, is over.[67] People have stopped pretending there is separation where none exists. There are only variations of form of one, whole dynamic information system. Therapy is communication — the dynamic exchange of information within a multidimensional world of information in motion. The therapy process is part of an ongoing, dynamic exchange of information.

68. Therapy is a conscious experience

Therapy requires that everyone involved be aware of what is going on. Once we accept that the universe is conscious, matter and energy take their form within hyperspacial networks of entangled spinners of information. Every person is part of this consciousness network. Therapy offers an inclusive environment – one that includes the right to be conscious, to participate in conscious conversations and an exchange of information between conscious participants, person-to-person, about real issues. Anything less than this limits the completeness of one's therapy process and likewise limits its potential therapeutic value. Therapists do not pretend to be therapeutic. Limited consciousness happens sometimes to everyone but therapists can do something about it — every time it happens.[68] They can tune in, reconnect, remember who they are and become present. Therapists are responsible for being conscious. They model a conscious reality.

69. Therapy is a multidimensional conversation

The state of being present conveys highly complex inflections. Within each conversation are enfolded messages of familiarity and comfort. We "resonate" even to those who cannot understand the words. One mechanism in which presence manifests itself is in the voice. The voice is the basis of a therapeutic conversation. The human voice is natural, not contrived; open, rather than rehearsed; and personal rather than professional. It carries information rather than prescriptions. But a state of being present is conveyed by a number of other mechanisms, as well. It resonates from holodynes within one's microtubules. This hidden dimension of consciousness also carries the therapeutic message – directly from the therapist's holodynes to the holodynes of others. Ultimately, therapy is a personal conversation between the Full Potential Self of one person and the Full Potential Self of another. Therapy is a multidimensional conversation.[69]

70. Therapy is an alignment

It is not the fancy office, the degree, the fame or the new book that impresses people. They have a natural confidence in a therapist who is aligned with the whole dynamic. The real information, the kind that is therapeutic, is information transmitted from a state of being aware of what is going on in the real world – including the hyperspacial quantum information fields of one's Full Potential Self. Therapy occurs when the therapist and the people involved are aligned with not only the situations of daily life, but with each other's Full Potential Selves.[70] Without this alignment, there can be no frequency transmitted that will bring coherence. There can be no unfolding of the potential and no therapeutic movement. All the dialogues in the world cannot compensate for one moment of holodynamic alignment.

71. Therapy is collaborative

Life is collaborative. Our increased intimacy with nature shows the fascinating network by which life survives and thrives synergistically. In order to sustain itself, life has demonstrated millions of years of collaborative efforts. Human life is just one example of complex collaboration. The entire biosphere is a living demonstration of how complex the collaboration of life has become.[71] Therapy is life-generating, naturally collaborative and inclusive. Therapy includes those with whom we relate, our partners, families and communities. It also includes collaboration with nature and with life itself. Therapists have joined the ranks of those who collaborate.

72. Therapy is a family affair — a living, intimate Being of Togetherness

Relationships have their own unique information network. These networks are made of self-contained holodynes that have the power to cause. Such holodynes form a "Being of Togetherness" (BOT) that manages relationships.[72] Since therapy is the experience of creating well-being at every level of consciousness, therapy also deals with those information systems that make up relationships between people. Each relationship develops its own personality and causal potency. It is self-surviving, has an order of growth and, like all holodynes, and is passed on from one generation to the next.

Family and cultural experiences reinforce these patterns of relating. Therapy nurtures the BOT. One purpose of therapy is to produce a healthy BOT between the therapist and the participant(s). This helps each relationship reach its fullest potential. When necessary, the therapy process transforms the BOT so that genuine intimacy results. Genuine intimacy is the natural byproduct of a healthy Being of Togetherness and is essential to psychological well-being. Therapy is inclusive. It cannot be conducted in isolation from the reality of family dynamics. Therapy is a family affair.

73. Therapy is a community activity

Holodynes embedded within the community become part of the culture, religious tradition and social belief systems of society. These holodynes are entangled in larger information fields held collectively by past generations and reinforced by social and cultural traditions. Therapy facilitates the shifting of such information fields through processes such as "*Re-living*. This process accesses transgenerational collective holodynes and, where necessary, transforms them.[73] Many collective holodynes contain information held as vital by our ancestors. It is the basis of our instincts and survival skills as a human race. They are part of the community. To change one such holodyne is to influence the entire field. Therapy is a community activity.

74. Therapy is life-enhancing

Our war with nature is over. Every form of life is driven by the same potential field of information that drives humans.[74] The driving potential, hidden within the quantum potential field of any given moment in time, contains the Full Potential Self of each life form. Our lives are nested within this field. It is inconsistent to believe that human therapy can occur without our "nest" of nature. Our biospheric balance is interwoven. Therapy is the alignment of the conscious person with his or her Full Potential Self and that brings into alignment all other potential emerging through the quantum potential field of life. We live in a morphogenic field. Everything is developing.

Therapy aligns people with life. This is far too complex for any linear mind to figure out. It is a process of constant communication with everyone and everything involved. Hyperspacial quantum fields provide information from past, present and future experiences, as well as all the possibilities of parallel worlds. Therapists who understand this reality are able to facilitate extraordinary experiences that create extraordinary results in therapeutic movement because they can access information from beyond the confines of space and time. Therapy is connected to all life in all its dimensions of consciousness. Therapy is life-enhancing.

75. Therapy is a balancing act

Which came first, internal or external balance? Is it possible they could both occur at one and the same moment — outside of time? Therapists, as normal humans, almost have to "get out of the way" and "let it happen." The natural state of life is to exist in a balanced biosphere. The biosphere is self-balancing because of its hyperspacial network of information fields. These fields are collective. They are engaged in quantum computing and constantly connected to every subatomic particle, every molecule and every living thing on earth. This network is so complex and magnificent it reflects a life-balancing process that is only barely breached and hardly understood by science today.[75]

Therapy recognizes this interconnection probability and facilitates conscious awareness of each person's possible part in the orchestration of life. Therapy is not an isolated event. It is a state of being in harmony. Internally and external balance begins within our own internal biosphere, among our holodynes. How can people expect to accomplish anything in the world unless they are responsible within their own inner world? The informed therapist understands global survival is connected to personal survival and accepts the potential that drives the therapy process. It's a balancing act.

76. Therapy ends when more than one conversation is taking place

When the therapist has one conversation "about people" behind closed doors, with a "command-and-control" administrator, the act itself reinforces a bureaucracy that is tripping over some cultural paranoia. Paranoia kills the "living" conversation. There is only one conversation that can create a win-win for everyone. That is the conversation among equals about our common state of being.[76]

77. Therapy explores beyond the firewalls of command and control

People love to be alive, conscious and connected – to be real. Everyone is formed and adheres to the laws of nature via spinner entanglements. Everyone and everything is symbiotically interwoven in the same information field. People can no longer afford to think of "conquest" of their fellow humans, or of "conquering" nature, destroying forests, over-fishing streams and oceans, or depleting the ozone layer. It is collective suicide. To remember our relationship with each other and with nature is to become collaborative. When we forget, we cause nature to falter and get sick and, in return, nature will cause us to falter and get sick. Nature has the power to cause.[77]

Therapy moves beyond our culturally obsolete notions of command and control that create "firewalls" between people and nature. It also moves beyond the firewall between the therapist and the people. Holodynes — all information — has a positive intent. Information is our "friend. Nature is our ally. There is nothing to war against. There is nothing to control or command. Only to explore and understand so, by sharing information therapists can facilitate those changes necessary to insure we unfold our fullest potential. This is the essence of nature and the essence of natural therapy.

78. Therapy is integration

The multidimensional nature of reality creates an ongoing invitation for cross-pollination of information from each dimension. Therapy is an invitation to integrate. Integration is healing, balancing and creates alignment. Once therapists move beyond the confines of linear analysis, treatment prescriptions and emotive processes, therapy becomes an intuitive presence.[78] Therapists, like physicists, mathematicians, biologists, chemists and even business and government leaders, are becoming informed about multidimensional dynamics and the healing power of integration. This includes the exploration of parallel dimensions, multiple histories, as well as past and future dynamics, as related to what is going on now. The integration of this information works in therapy and in life.

79. Therapy is the "emerging" of a new state of being

Information has, inherent within itself, an emerging potential. Life is not dependent only upon Darwin's law of natural survival. Life "emerges" from the quantum potential field. Each life form and each set of circumstances in which we find ourselves, are the by-product of complex hyperspacial computations that are "entangled" in such a way that we are able to "reduce" all those possibilities into our defined reality, and allow for a new state of being to emerge. In other words, the quantum field "collapses" into this reality according to an implicate order determined by the computations performed in hyperspace and by our own free will.[77]

All information, including information systems that create chaos in thinking, is subject to free choice. "By choice!" and not just the therapist's choice alone. Therapy is a total experience including both the therapist and the participant(s). It is designed so as to meet the requirements of this implicate order and allow for the emergence of new consciousness. By choice, the hyperspacial field collapses and a new state of being emerges.

80. Therapy is a process

Therapy is a process. It is the process of unfolding potential. This potential emerges according to built in patterns that span each stage of a person's life cycle. These patterns are part of an implicate order contained within the quantum field. Developmental psychology is dedicated to identifying these patterns and establishing the process by which people develop from one stage to the next in their life cycle. These stages can be summarized into six natural stages of development.[80] The person emerges first as a physical being. Next a personality begins to develop. Soon relationships develop and then social systems emerge and maintain themselves. The process continues as living principles manifest and finally the person develops a universal grasp of reality. The process is always multidimensional, bounded to the past, present and future, and always reflecting the hidden dimensions of consciousness, such as holodynes, parallel worlds and the implicate order. The process cannot be limited to behavioral modification or rationalism. It is non-linear, quantum and holodynamic. Therapy reflects the natural process of development.

81. The old therapy doesn't work anymore

Therapy has moved beyond the idea of "illusions," "delusions," "episodes" or "schizophrenia. Therapy reaches into any active information field and creates change. It does not matter whether the holodynes are from the past, present or future. It does not matter if the cause comes from this world or from parallel worlds. The therapist's new understanding of the nature of reality has ended past centuries of psychiatric elitism and hidden atrocities. Some of our most gifted conscious humans have been tortured, electro-shocked, drugged out of consciousness, or confined and separated from society simply because our theoretical frameworks and treatment modalities were inadequate. In light of the new knowledge, an informed public no longer tolerates such incompetence but demands treatment modalities that create better results and are based on the latest findings from all sources of knowledge. Inadequacies or outright violations, due to ignorance, as in the past, are made public immediately on the Internet. The secret closets of the mental hospitals and private offices, where abuse of those labeled "mentally ill" once took place, are now uncovered. The public is an informed one and insists that therapy adopt those information fields that create lasting mental health and psychological well-being.[81]

82. The therapist talks with people at their own level

When the therapist gets down and talks with people, eye-to-eye, and heart-to-heart, all the special language slung around at conventions or learned special courses drops away. This complex language has nothing to do with people. When people hear it, their eyes glaze over and everything goes on remote control. Therapy cannot be conducted from remote control. The people are not "in" the faceless books or the endless reports from various professional journals. It is the *people* who need to be heard. It is their *state of being* that needs to be read. Therapy talks *directly* to people. People talk directly to a therapist. People want to be *embraced* by therapy and they will embrace therapy in return. A therapist will talk with people on their level.[82]

83. People know things too

People have their own tools. They have their own sense of reality. They have experienced their own senses of the human body, both sending and receiving information. They may not know the words as their fine-grained and gross-grained screens manage their perception but they can sense a deeper reality, a quantum network responsible for their own coherence and well-being. They are connected.[83] Therapists do not underestimate people. They know that those Frohlech frequencies pick up the nurturing that is needed in therapy. It is a message that no rational, analytical or contrived treatment program, no drugs, machines or isolation procedures can transmit. The state of being a therapist transmits psychological well-being. The therapist establishes coherence and the people know it.

84. Therapy is co-authorship

People co-author their own development. The emergence of consciousness over time is entangled with the Full Potential Self of every life form. The quantum computations in hyperspaciality are operating in the fullness of time, non-linearly, in parallel with all time sequences at once. Thus each species that emerges over time is interconnected with all other species that come before or follow afterward any specific event. Evolution occurs as a time sequence in the physical world but, in the quantum field, evolution is co-authored by choices made collectively, by that collective potential driving any given situation.[84]

The Full Potential of every life form is the co-author of every manifestation of life. Therapy facilitates the creation of coherence among the network of Full Potential Selves that have co-authored the evolution of consciousness within a person, a family or a society, of humanity – of all life. Therapy is the experience of co-authoring one's own evolution of consciousness. The therapist no longer see the "patient" or "client" as "getting well," but rather as co-authorship of a chosen, emerging state of being. This turns out to be a lot more satisfying and more therapeutic for everyone.

85. Therapy reflects our symbiotic relationship to reality

Reality is symbiotic. Space, time, matter and life are in symbiotic relationship. Screens, both fine-grained and gross-grained, cover all our senses. These screens facilitate our holographic experience of reality. When the screens change, our experience changes accordingly. Our screens are controlled by holodynes that are bonded to our Full Potential Self. We are locked into a perception of time and space by a pre-conscious computational system from which emerges our experience with reality. Life is symbiotically connected throughout this universal field of computations and our perception screens.[85] Therapy facilitates the "remembering" of a field of consciousness that cannot be completely evolved until, by free will choice, its component potential parts emerge as coherent and symbiotic beyond the control of our perception screens. We are interwoven inseparably into our symbiotic relationship with reality.

86. Therapy is unique

No two information systems are the same. This uniqueness is timeless. Therapy reveres and preserves this uniqueness. A therapist does not classify people into categories and treat them according to a prescribed group format. It cannot be done because no two sets of circumstances are ever the same. Like snowflakes, the moment you might think they are the same, the field shifts by the touch of your consciousness, and they are not the same. Therapy is never the same; the field shifts by the touch of your own consciousness, and they are not the same.[86] Therapy is never the same, moment by moment, day by day, or person by person. Therapists and their insurance companies must get over the habit of allowing classifications to determine therapy. It is counter-therapeutic.

87. Therapy maintains a "superposition"

Reality is not confined to time and space. It cannot be contained in one school of thought. Nor can it be confined to one experience, one moment in time, one individual's interpretation of experience or one group's translation of events. Reality, and thus therapy, embraces and is embraced by Holodynamics. There is no "one way" to lead, interact or control events.

Consciousness is dynamic, emerging from and in constant feedback with hyperspacial dynamics.[87] Therapy is dynamic and is constant reformation. Every subatomic particle, every molecule, microtubule, cell and organ of the body, including the human brain and neural system, is in constant relationship with hyperspacial information fields. Every situation in a person's life is driven by its counterpart in hyperspace for the purpose of unfolding the dynamic life potential of that individual. Our definition of reality dictates our definition of therapy. When a therapist judges our actions, referees our games, or takes over, the therapist becomes part of our problem.

Even if the problem seems linear, therapy cannot be contained within a linear model. Reality is also non-linear and hyperspacial. Models of reality, leadership, education, health and psychotherapy must embrace all dimensions of reality in order to be comprehensive. In order to do this, the therapist must remain in "superposition" — inclusive but beyond being drawn into the downdraft dynamics of the situation. Therapy must remain inclusive and in superposition in order to remain effective.

FOOTNOTES - CHAPTER TWELVE

66. The Covenant: Refers to the hyperspacial promise, made by choice, beyond the confines of space and time. This "promise" is unique for each person and each group. It is both individual and collective and is interwoven into the matrix of consciousness of the universe (see Bohm, Penrose, Hameroff, Hawking, Woolf, 2005). It is not confined to space or time, nor is it considered sequential. Rather, it is a living condition of involvement, continual choice, and unfolding potential.

67. Exchange: The universe is made of information in motion. Reality exists because it is formed from a constant exchange of information. Human life, including the therapy process, is always a dynamic exchange of information. Anything considered less than this is a downdraft dynamic and therefore cannot be considered part of therapy (see Woolf, 2005).

68. Consciousness: The state of awareness of one's reality. In the Townsend model (See Hawking, 2001), there are at least 10 dimensions enfolded within reality. Similarly, there is at least that number of dimensions enfolded within consciousness.

69. A multidimensional conversation: See footnote 76 for references to "conversation. "Multidimensional" refers to the enfolded dimensions of consciousness (see Woolf, 2005, and footnotes 1-14). All communication is multidimensional.

70. Alignment: In electronics, messages are only able to be transmitted via wire or airwaves, if they are "in alignment" with both the sender and receiver. The introduction of quantum physics into the field of therapy has opened the door to new understanding of how certain frequencies carry the messages of consciousness. The messages of consciousness require alignment the same as all other frequencies (Woolf, 2005).

71. Collaboration: Refers to acts of cooperation or the state of being in cooperation with others. See *Leadership and Teambuilding: the Holodynamics of Birthing a New World: Manual IV*, Woolf, 2006.

72. Being of Togetherness: Refer to Woolf 1990 and *Field Shifting, the Holodynamics of Integration, Manual III*, 2001, 2006.

73. Community activity: Refers to collective activities of people. All such activities reflect collective consciousness. Refer to Kelly, 1995, and Woolf, 2005, for more details.

74. Life-enhancing: All matter and all living things are made of "quantum foam" (see *Parallel Universes,* Fred Alan Wolf, 1990). Within this foam are micro (small) "white holes" and "black holes." White holes are life-enhancing while black holes are life-diminishing. In Holodynamic Psychology, this is referred to as "updraft" and "downdraft" dynamics (Woolf, 1990). Specific behavioral patterns have been identified from various schools of thought. These behavioral patterns emerge at each stage of development. Each pattern has an updraft and a downdraft dynamic (Woolf, 1990, page 48). While it may be argued that both updraft and downdraft dynamics are interwoven into reality, life-enhancing processes are updraft. Thus, at any given moment in time, each person has choice between updraft or downdraft, life or death. (See footnote 18).

75. Balancing act: As children, who among us has not marveled when, at the circus, those amazing men and women on the high trapeze, walked along the wire doing their balancing act? Therapy is like that. It is a balancing of rational, emotional and holodynamic reality. It is a balancing of the daily pressures of the physical world, compared to emotional and imagined realities, intermingled with complex interchange with parallel worlds (see "Topological Mind Model" in Woolf, 1990). The key to balance is always found in holodynamic dimension of "presence." (See footnotes 8, 9, 10 and 11).

76. Conversation: There are three process dimensions into which information channels itself within the human body. The first is linear. The second is wave, and the third is presence (Woolf, 2005).

An analytical conversation (as when a therapist "consults" with another colleague "about" a "patient") is a linear process. All linear processes require separation. The therapist is positioned "in a command and control" position. The participant is now a "patient." The conversation is "about" another person. As soon as the therapist shifts into any linear process, therapy ends. It can go "on hold" and the process by which therapy moves forward to create well-being, stops (Woolf, 2005).

What, then, is "command and control?" Intuitively (from "presence"), the therapist understands the process has stopped. Yet, in order to defend the entropy (the dysfunction in the therapy process), the therapist allows a matrix to be created around the inertia (slowdown). The defense matrix is filled with hidden holodynes that perpetuate the blocked therapy process. These are "command and control" practices, policies and procedures that have become part of the infrastructure of therapy. Too bad. It has nothing to do with therapy. It has to do with creating a "secure" therapy process that, by its very nature, is the embodiment of dysfunction in the therapy process. One way out of this collective oxymoron is to include the participant in any consultation with any other professional, colleague or staff or other consultant. (See footnotes 77, 80, and 81).

77. Firewalls: From a military frame of reference, "firewall" is a defense wall against the oncoming enemy. In computer language, "firewalls" refer to defensive blocks against hackers or intruders. This defensive language has intruded into the field of therapy. In therapy, a "firewall" exists when the therapist seeks an alliance with colleagues outside of the therapy relationship. This alliance may be a professional consultation with other therapists, pharmaceutical professional, or staff members. This alliance allows the therapist to block intrusions into the therapy process. But who is "the intruding enemy?" It is the "patient" – the one who has placed trust in the therapist. (See Carse, *Finite and Infinite Games*, 1994).

78. Integration: Complex information systems have a natural built-in order by which information can be integrated. This system involves all dimensions of reality (see Woolf, 2005). One dimension, for example, is the hyperspacial dimension where pre-computations exist (Hawking,

2001; Penrose, 1997) from which a person gains conscious access to one's Full Potential Self. Another is creative imagination (Woolf, 1990) following the Place of Peace process of "round-tabling" (Woolf, 1990).

79. The "emerging" state of being: In both mathematics and physics, it is evident that everything has a hyperspacial counterpart (Hawking, Woolf 2005; footnotes 1-14). Psychology and related fields of therapy have been slow to apply this information to human consciousness, which is a primary reason for this treatise.

80. Process: The process of therapy is another dimension of therapy. Many participants seldom, if ever, think of the process of therapy. But consciousness emerges from hyperspace (see footnotes 1-14) according to an implicate order (see footnotes 15, 35 and 66 for further references).

81. Old Therapies: Any therapy system that has not adapted itself to the new information now available, is by its lack of action, an "old" therapy. These "old" therapies do not work anymore because people are facing new challenges. In the "good old days," it was a major challenge to get off the farm and into town. In an agricultural society, people had to know all about horses, wagons, rough roads and the like. Then the Industrial Revolution brought the majority of the population into cities. Jobs changed. Society changed. New technology sprang into every person's life.

We became a mobile generation. People became mobile. They could fly all around the planet in machines never dreamed of by their grandparents. Most of this new population stopped producing food or machines. They became involved in information and services exchange and became glued to the computer, e-mail and Internet. These changes occurred relatively quickly and this new age required new skills and new types of knowledge.

Therapy has become, for many people, their best hope of finding coherence in this new age. Therapy can, if it reaches its potential, help people better understand high technologies, work in complex environments, adjust to global mobility, manage overloads of information from new cultures, and adjust to flexible infrastructures. Therapy can provide a way to manage instant communication, mass media intrusiveness, depersonalized economic maneuverings, spiritual commercialization and political artistry, to mention a few. Old therapies cannot survive unless they adapt. (See *Leadership and Teambuilding: the Holodynamics of Birthing a New World: Manual IV*, Woolf, 2006).

82. On their level: Therapy begins within the event horizon of the information system that is in charge of the person's state of being. This does not mean the therapist gives up his or her own sense of reality. It does mean the therapist extends his or her own consciousness to embrace the others. In a world of many cultures and beliefs, the therapist's job is to begin "on their level," gaining access to their information systems. Only then can therapy be conducted. (See footnote 83 for more references).

83. People know things: While this statement may appear self-evident, there are many social and theocratic outlooks that suggest exactly the opposite. Most pyramids of power are built upon the assumption that the collective "people" are not as informed as the "elite." Science, however, finds that information is always connected in some dimension of reality (Bohm). Furthermore, the mechanisms or consciousness are set to transmit and receive information Holodynamically (Woolf, 2005), i.e., in every dimension of consciousness. See footnotes 1-14 for more references. In the area of therapy, special knowledge is possessed by the therapist but almost all of it is irrelevant to therapy. See footnotes 64, 66, 76 and 77 for clarification.

84. Co-authorship: In books like Guy Murchie's *The Seven Mysteries of Life*, it is evident that all manner of life forms exist as the result of co-authorship. Ants, for example, that live within certain trees, protect the tree from parasites and being fed sap from special nipples. Birds that spread seeds of the fruit they eat and bacteria that digest food in the stomach are a few common examples. Other books, such as Jon Luoma's *The Hidden Forest* (1999) point out how complex co-authorship and mutual symbiosis becomes in life.

85. Symbiosis: refers to "synergy in biological systems" or "extra energy from synapse." Nature is replete with examples of symbiosis. For thousands of examples, see Guy Murchie, *The Seven Mysteries of Life*. The evidences from physics are also numerous. Read David Bohm and David Peate for quantum examples; refer to Penrose, 1994, for specific examples of symbiosis in consciousness. For examples of symbiosis in therapy, see Woolf, 2005.

86. Uniqueness: The fact that everything is made of information in motion reveals a reality that is always dynamic (Penrose 1994; Hawking, 2001). The fact that reality is holographic in form reveals a physical world with an endless array of shapes and colors (Talbot). The fact that the universe is conscious reveals a dynamic, endless array of experiences that, from the dimension of holodynes, take on an endless array of shape, color, form and experience (Woolf, 2005). Every set of circumstances is driven by potential (Bohm et al, 1987) and thus therapy is always a unique experience.

87. The "superposition" of therapy: Literally every therapy school of thought gives reference to maintaining a therapeutic "superposition. Usually, this state of being is referred to as "remaining objective," maintaining "positive regard," or "psychological distance," "managing transference" or "avoiding duality," or some other label. It is rarely, if ever, referred to in the light of an actual holodynamic state of being, interwoven with every dimension of reality (see treatises 1-14, 85, 90, and 91 for more references).

CHAPTER THIRTEEN

THE RESULTS OF THERAPY

*T*HE RESULTS OF THERAPY

88. Psychological well-being

Once we realize that the "business of life" is an ongoing experience regarding the unfolding of some aspect of life potential, then we can view the outcome of all our actions as a reflection of our life potential. The business of therapy becomes "to identify the updraft or downdraft exchanges within the information field." Any action can be viewed as adding to, or taking from, one's unfolding potential. When we "plan ahead" for example, such "planning" will not unfold potential if it is confined to a linear thinking and/or emotional/wave process.[88]

It must include the whole dynamic and make room for hyperspacial occurrences that compute menus of options, share information, and provide integrative influences. This "alliance" with the whole dynamic is essential in the unfolding of potential. One cannot impose a singular planned event upon a hyperspacial quantum field. It is the positive intent of the hyperspacial field that is reflected into each set of circumstances. Thus our deepest intention deserves our fullest attention. The outcome of any self-organizing information system is always driven by intention. The intended result is the unfolding of potential. Therapy is driven by holodynamic intention and alignment with this intention creates psychological well-being.

89. Integrated swarm intelligence

The birds do it; the bees do it; and humans do it. We exhibit "swarm" intelligence, or collective consciousness. Swarm intelligence can better be understood when consciousness is viewed through the holographic principle. The holographic principle states that "What is known to the part is known to the whole and what is known to the whole is known to the part.[89]

Life is not about the part dominating the whole or the whole dominating the part. From this view, dictatorial tyrants or groups are a thing of the past. The world is in a transition toward co-creation of the transformation of consciousness into universal collaboration. Therapy reflects, in philosophy and practice, the experience of co-creation. It is part of the emergence of a communicating, collaborative community that includes every life form on the planet, as well as every person and every set of circumstances. It is the recognition that life is in constant communication, hyperspacially and locally. Therapy is "real" and invites others to become real and join the party. Therapy utilizes swarm intelligence.

90. Coherence

Psychological heath is the byproduct of coherence. Coherence occurs when one's information systems come into synchronicity. Information systems seek this harmonic state of being. When multidimensional, non-linear experiences are identified as "holy" events, both the source and the participant(s) are soon distanced and divinized by linear thinkers who are trying to relate the events. This linear action allows rational thinkers the justification for their limited consciousness. They form a theology, philosophy, ideology, or a set of beliefs about the events in order to confine the experiences within a "set" framework. This process creates a "closed" information system, or an "event horizon," that "contains" the hyperspacial dynamics within a confined mentality. While this tends to make linear thinkers "safe," it also provides the basis for so many religious, political, business (and other) atrocities. This type of thinking has been perpetuated upon the human race for thousands of years of recorded history and still plagues humankind in our modern age.[90]

"Good" and "evil," for example, are labels placed upon dynamics over which one has achieved a limited conscious understanding. It is limited because it is locked within a polarized set of holodynes usually interacting within a closed event horizon. Once understood from a holodynamic view, all human behavior has inherent value. Consciousness is holodynamic. To focus on spiritual things is simply to focus on hyperspacial things and does not justify dominance. Therapy often requires focusing on issues related to values, ethics, social interaction, self-definition and other issues that are intimately entwined with hyperspacial/space-time coherence. Everything is coherent in some dimension of reality. The purpose of therapy is to reestablish coherence and restore psychological well-being.

91. Personal superposition

One of the capabilities of consciousness is the ability to be engaged or not, to be present or not, at the same time. Like a quantum computer that is both "on" and "off" at the same time, people can be "at choice point" regarding any issue of their daily living. In a similar way, the therapist is always "on" regarding the therapy process and, at the same time, aspects of the process are always "off." Movement, in a therapeutic sense, can be facilitated through the process of "Tracking", "Re-living" and "Pre-living," as well-being is brought into coherence. These processes, like all aspects of therapy, are both "on" and "off," all the time. Like cable Internet services, they are available at the flick of a switch. Therapy results in people developing and maintaining the superposition, both "on" and "off" regarding problems and solutions.[91]

FOOTNOTES - CHAPTER THIRTEEN

88. Well-being: *The Dance of Life* (Woolf, 2005) and the five manuals that expand upon its basic findings, (Woolf 2005-6), outline in great detail the state of well-being for not only humans, but for all life on the planet. The presentations are from a holodynamic view.

89. Integrated swarm intelligence: See, for example, Kevin Kelly's report in *Out of Control.* Kelly notes that in high-speed photographic measurements of birds in flight, one bird sights a hawk. It takes $1/70^{th}$ of a second for the information, once the light hits the fovea of the bird's eye, to be transmitted through the optical nerve into the vision center of the brain and then be passed on to register "hawk = danger" in the microtubules. It takes an additional $1/70^{th}$ of a second for the holodyne that stores the memory of "hawk = danger" to signal the muscles and start avoidance procedures. The bird flies away from the hawk. The interesting thing to note it that the entire flock of birds responds at the same moment. They do not require the external "sight" of the hawk to fly away.

They react without the initial $1/70$ of a second wherein the information passes through the neural system. Birds have the ability to communicate instantly, from the holodyne of one bird to holodynes of all the others. The only explanation possible is that holodynes can communicate hyperspacially. The quantum potential field within microtubules provides a portal for information to be transmitted beyond the limits of time and space. Birds, fish, insects and other forms of life seem to demonstrate this ability.

90. Coherence: Refers to information waves that resonate with harmonic frequencies. This principle applies to biological systems in fields of superconductivity and superfluidity at normal biological temperatures (see Frohlech). It also applies to consciousness within biological systems (see Hawking, 2001; Hameroff, 1987; Penrose, 2000; and Woolf 2005). For references on event horizons, see Woolf, 2005 *Principle-driven Transformation: The Holodynamics of the Dance of Life, Manual V* and for references on "good and evil," refer to, Woolf, 1990.

91. Superposition: See Woolf and Blue, 2001. It is recognized that the field of quantum computers is still in its initial stages of development. The RICCI computer robot is an early version of what is possible (see RICCI). Since robots can maintain a "superposition" of being "on" and "off" at the same time, it is self-evident that humans can do the same in any type of situation. When this ability is practiced in a therapeutic setting, complex situations become much easier to handle.

CHAPTER FOURTEEN

THERAPY AS A PUBLIC TRUST

THERAPY AS A PUBLIC TRUST

92. What the future holds for Therapy

Therapy holds the key to the future psychological well-being of the planet. Imagine any person who chooses to establish psychological well-being and applies for therapy. Here is what is coming. That person, as a potential partner in therapy, will contact the therapist prior to entering therapy. The applicant will be thinking something like this: "Information is perceived and transmitted via a series of Frohlech frequencies. Frohlech frequencies are part of the holodynamic network responsible for the quantum coherence of the body and thus are involved in the coherence of consciousness. I am looking for a therapist who can resonate with the necessary quantum frequencies that nurture coherence. Can you provide such coherence?"

The applicant will know that specific conditions and states of being that are necessary for the therapist to be capable of transmitting such frequencies. They also will know that no corporate or professional, rational, analytical or contrived treatment program, nor any drugs, machines or isolation procedures, can transmit such frequencies. Neither can people who are mindless "resonators" of "energy"; those with "their heart on their sleeve" or "emotive" provide the services needed. They will be looking for help from a personal, present, knowledgeable therapist with the ability to transmit a holodynamic state of being the kind of coherence that produces therapeutic movement.[92]

They will want a practical, down-to-earth therapist. Modern clients know the therapist is vital to the therapy process and they want to be able to trust that the therapist will act appropriately and professionally from a holodynamic view. The future of therapy is limited only by the boundaries of our event horizons that we have placed upon the therapy field.

93. Therapists realize their potential markets are laughing at them

Like all public service agents, therapists realize their potential customers are often laughing at them. The public eye makes fun of everyone. Perhaps the most constructive approach is to laugh along with them but take their humor to heart. Enfolded within all ridicule are "diamonds" of truth "in the rough." The therapy process is for self-application. Besides, therapy is fun! The therapist can laugh – he or she must be able to maintain a sense of humor!

When confronted with ridicule, therapists need to lighten up, take themselves less seriously and enjoy the process.[93]

This does not mean the therapist can laugh *at* those in therapy or put jokes about them on the Internet. Rather, a sense of humor means the therapist remains "bigger than the situation," with values that can include people, maintain a little humility, provide straight talk and maintain a genuine point of view. Therapy is fun, exciting and life-generating.

94. Therapy is an open door

One way to tell if a therapist has an open mind is to see if he or she has an open door. Therapists are faced daily with a wide array of new information, new research and new ideas. In this Information Age, it is difficult, if not impossible, to stay abreast of new developments in technology, let alone the amazing breakthroughs in therapy that appear almost daily from various parts of the world. Add to this the necessity of dealing with professional colleagues, associates and other helping systems such as medical, insurance, political, religious and family influences. And these are only a few of the network of dynamic pressures in the field of therapy. Too often the therapist sets up a natural defense against accepting new information.

A "set of criteria" begins to form within the mind of the therapist. The first telltale signs of a closed door (and a closed mind) appear as the necessity to diagnose, classify and shuffle into "appropriate treatment" processes, or the desire to have a stable cash flow. The therapist puts his practice "on cruise control," where it is automated. Controlled by enfolded holodynes, the "real" therapist, or the holodynamic being, has "lost control." The result is potentially disastrous for therapy. The old and familiar practices become a closed network and therapy develops its own event horizon.[94]

To the degree that this happens, the therapy door closes. The entire information network of the therapist is contained within an event horizon. Under these circumstances, unless the applicant "fits," there can be no therapy. The therapy "door" is closed except to those who "comply." Real therapy however, is always an open door.

95. Therapy is a public trust

The public has entrusted the therapist to provide professional service and care for the psychological well-being of the people. The therapist is expected to study the various theories and modalities of therapy and to be able to professionally intervene in situations that require the services of a therapist. In order to keep this public trust, the therapist is required to remain current on pertinent information applicable to each person's consciousness and the processes for establishing psychological health.[95]

FOOTNOTES - CHAPTER FOURTEEN

92. The future: The author admits that this is only one alternative future and it may not apply to everyone. However, the fact remains that anyone can access the future – or the past (see Woolf, 2005).

93. The laughing marketplace: Referenced in www.cluetrainmanifesto.com the laughing marketplace is recognized in the world of business where, especially with the new influence of the Internet, the market is becoming more transparent and responsive to what is available in the way of services. For those who fail to represent themselves in a professional manner, the market responds with contempt. Therapists are not immune to such treatment and, as history shows, the profession has suffered in the public eye. Therapists, like any other service providers, must be responsive to market demands (see Woolf, 2005, 2006).

94. In reality, the door is always open: As people begin to understand that quantum computations hold all options at the same time, therapy becomes more "quantum" and more dynamic. Options held in hyperspace can be compared to a quantum computer that is both "on" and "off" at the same time. Necessary analysis and computations become non-linear. By the time a human being touches a key on the keyboard, the computer has waited an equivalent of 1,000 years for its next instructions. By the time a choice is made, our hyperspacial counterparts have waited much longer for us to make the choice. The human eye is capable of detecting a single photon. Thus, human sensory perception and consciousness itself is quantum in nature (see Woolf and Blue, 2001). Therapy is quantum.

95. Therapy is a public trust: The reason I mention this at the very end is to emphasize the need for therapists to keep current on the most recent findings from the various efforts of scientists around the world. Of particular interest are the findings from quantum physics, information theory, holographics, vortex energy and the science of consciousness. This treatise is focused on the implications and applications of these new findings to the practice of therapy.

FURTHER NOTES:

Those familiar with history will recognize the similarity between these 95 Treatises and the 95 Treatises that Martin Luther nailed to the church door in the 14th century. His document outlined the teachings of the Bible compared to the practices of the Catholic Church and sparked the Protestant revolution. A similar type of document on business practices may be found in the Clue Train Manifesto, available under www.//cluetrain.com on the Internet. The Clue Train's 95 Treatises reflect the revolutionary impact of the Internet on the principles and practice of doing business around the world.

Likewise, this "Therapy Manifesto" and its "95 Treatises on Holodynamic Therapy," reflect the revolutionary findings of the sciences of quantum physics, information theory, holographics, quantum computing, superconductivity, biophysics, developmental psychology, neurology, vortex energy and telecommunications, to mention a few. These revolutionary findings shed new light on human consciousness and contain profound implications for therapists. This manifesto also brings to light more than 30 years of research in the application of these new perspectives and their transformative impact upon the principles and practices of therapy and of society' search for emotional, mental and spiritual well-being.

More information on this "Therapy Manifesto and the 95 Treatise on Holodynamic Therapy" can be found on the Internet at www.holodynamics.com or by e-mail: academy@holodynamics.com

GLOSSARY OF TERMS

Being of Togetherness (BOT)

The information matrix that controls relationships.

Being of System's Synergy (BOSS)

The information matrix that controls systems and organizations.

Black hole

A region of space where, in traditional thought, nothing can escape because the gravity is so strong. From a holographic view, a black hole stores information and radiates it out in subtle mass exchanges. Thought processes give indications of being influenced by similar dynamics when they become "downdrafted".

Boundary Condition

The initial state of a physical system or the state of the system at some boundary in space-time. Consciousness organizes into fields of information that develop specific boundary conditions.

Brane

An object that appears to be a fundamental ingredient of M-theory that can have a variety of spatial dimensions. In general, a p-brane is a length in p direction; a 1-brane is a string; a 2-brane is a surface or a membrane, etc. In the science of consciousness, the p-brane model is useful to distinguish between fundamental ingredients that make up identifiable or unique aspects of systems of consciousness.

Biophysics

The study of the physical laws governing biological systems and their interconnection with the mechanisms of consciousness.

Brane World

The world as we experience it through our senses is considered a 4-brane world of depth, height, width and time. Hyperspacial worlds are considered to have more dimensions than this world and, at the same time, all dimensions are intimately interwoven with each other.

Causal potency

The power to cause, as in biological and neuron-chemical reactions, that control body functions or holodynes that control biology, thoughts, feelings and states of being.

Classical Theory

A theory based upon concepts established prior to relativity or quantum mechanics. Classical Theory assumes that objects have well-defined positions and velocities. This is not true on very small scales, such as in consciousness, where the Heisenberg principle applies and motion and velocity cannot be measured at the same time.

Conservation of Energy

The law of nature that demonstrates that energy (or its equivalent in mass) cannot be created or destroyed. This law appears to apply to all forms of consciousness.

Cosmological Constant

A mathematical device used by Einstein to give the universe a built-in tendency to expand and allowed the theory of relatively to predict a static universe. Einstein stated that this was his "biggest error," but research indicates that consciousness may in fact, be the cosmological constant he was seeking.

Cosmology

The study of the universe as a whole and referred to in these writings as "Holodynamics."

Counterpart

Defines a one-to-one holographic relationship between states in our four-dimensional world and states in higher dimensions.

Curled-up Dimension

A special dimension that is curved up so small it can escape detection by our holographic sensory perception screen.

Collective consciousness

Also known as "swarm intelligence" among insects, fish, birds and other species including humans. This ability is demonstrated when more than one person shares a similar state of consciousness with others.

Dark Matter

Matter in galaxies and clusters and space that cannot be observed directly but can be detected by its gravitational field. More than 97% of the matter in the universe is considered to be composed of dark matter.

Developmental Psychology

The study of how humans grow and change during the course of their lives. Explores all aspects of human development from conception to old age. Identifies the stages of development of emerging consciousness.

Dimension

A measurable coordinate in one unique direction as in the four dimensions of space-time (breadth, height, width and time). It is hypothesized that there are at least ten dimensions enfolded within the measurement of gravity. Refer to p-brane.

DNA

Deoxyribonucleic acid, composed of phosphate, a sugar, and four bases: adenine, guanine, thymine and cytosine. Two strands of DNA form a double helix structure that resembles a spiral staircase. Construction process seems to be orchestrated by spinners that appear from hyperspace. DNA encodes all the information cells require to reproduce and plays a vital role in heredity.

Duality

A correspondence between apparently different theories that lead to the same physical results.

Electromagnetic Force

The force that arises between particles with electric charges of similar or opposite sign (positive or negative).

Emotional processing

The capacity of information systems to function according to non-linear dynamics as demonstrated through emotions such as love, hate, elation and depression. Equated to "wave" dynamics because the process resembles the way waves behave.

Enfolded dimensions

An object that appears to be a fundamental ingredient of M-theory that can have a variety of special dimensions as in p-branes.

Entropy

A measure of the disorder of a physical system, the number of different microscopic configurations of a system that leave its macroscopic appearance unchanged.

Event

A point in space-time.

Event Horizon

The boundary of any given information system — as in the boundary of a black hole — beyond which it is impossible to escape. Applies to any conscious system beyond which one cannot conceive of any other view.

Field

Something that exists throughout space and time (as apposed to a particle event that exists within a given point): applies to states of consciousness that are collectively held among more than one holodyne or more than one individual.

Fine-grained screens

Identified by Karl Pribram as closely meshed fabrics that cover all of the senses. Fine-grained screens are thought to be information filters associated with particle data systems involved in holographic information exchange as in the fovea of the eye or the cilia of the ear.

Force Field

The means by which a force communicates its influence: as among humans, when an ideal is held in common and associated with certain boundaries or held within specific limits.

Frequency

For a wave: the number of complete cycles per second.

Frohlech frequencies

Named for Herbert Frohlech who, in 1968, predicted that a quantum frequency would be discovered that allowed coherence within the human body. The frequency (approximately 10 to the minus 33 per second) is found in microtubules and thought be central in the communication of information along neural passages, among cells, and between organs of the body.

General Relativity

Einstein's theory based upon the idea that the laws of science should be the same for all observers, no matter how they are moving. It explains the force of gravity in terms of the curvature of a found-dimensional space-time. Sometimes used in the exploration of the movement of information fields of consciousness.

Genomics

The study of genetic codes, the DNA, gene splicing and cloning and applied to the study of inherited holodynes and collective fields of consciousness.

Grand Unification Theory

A theory that seeks to unify the electromagnetic, strong and weak forces and used in the exploration of the nature of consciousness.

Gross-grained screens

Loosely meshed fabrics that cover all of the senses and are thought to be information filters associated with wave data systems involved in holographic information exchange. The periphery of the eye and the ear drum are examples of gross-grained screens that perform a holographic function in perception.

Holographic Theory

The idea that the quantum states of a system in a region of space-time may be encoded on the boundary of that region allowing more complex systems to be projected upon a simpler system. From this view, humans are considered to be projections from a more complex system into the space-time continuum where they are manifesting the complex system (hyperspacial counterparts) through the simple system (physical bodies).

Hologram

A three-dimensional image projected onto a two-dimensional object as in a three-dimensional picture, projected onto a page. Holograms can be multiple-dimensional information systems contained within a lesser-dimensioned space-time. From this view, a human being is considered to have a holographic nature.

Holodyne

Information systems stored in holographic form in the water media of the microtubules. From "holo" meaning "whole" and "dyne" meaning "unit of power," as in "dynamite" or "dynamo." Holodynes are considered holographic thought forms that have the power to cause and thus have been identified as being in control of most human thoughts, feelings and behavior.

Holodynamic

A school of thought that includes the exploration of all dimensions of reality, including all dimensions of consciousness.

Holodynamic Therapy

The theory and practice of therapy that includes the whole dynamic of reality. This approach views reality as conscious, dynamic, multidimensional and interconnected, as outlined in these treatises and other texts as referenced.

Holographic matrix

The information field that gives form to everything. Not confined to the space-time continuum but inclusive (see M-theory).

Holographic screens

Sensory screens (refer to fine-grained and gross-grained screens) used in holographic information exchange (see holodynes).

Hyperspace

A dimension of reality beyond the confines of three-dimensional space and time.

Hyperspacial counterpart

The holographic phenomenon of a one-to-one relationship between information networks of spinners (herein referred to as "the Full Potential Self" of each individual) beyond the confines of space-time (thus hyperspace) that are pre-computing the quantum potential sets within every set of circumstances in space-time.

Hyperspacial information spinners

A faster-than-light, quantum potential field, identified by Roger Penrose as "made of networks of information systems" in vortex motion, that are "pre-computing" all possibilities for "every set of circumstances" in space-time (see Full Potential Self).

Implicate order

One of the basic tenants of quantum physics, first proposed by David Bohm, which presents the fundamental idea that beyond the visible, tangible world there lies a deeper, implicate order of undivided wholeness. Life and consciousness "emerge" in space-time according to a built-in order.

Information

Literally, "in-forms" or holographic spinners that are projected from a more complex system into a less complex system. Anything that has a pattern is considered "in form" and made of information. Everything we can sense is made of information.

Information Theory

A series of theorems about communication systems first developed by Claude Shannon, starting from the source coding theorem, which uses entropy as the measure of information and culminating in the noisy channel coding theorem, including codes for data compression and error correction. The principles of information theory are used in the study of consciousness.

Interference Pattern

The wave pattern that appears from the merging of two or more waves that are emitted from different locations or at different times. Used in the study of consciousness to indicate conflicting information systems.

Linear thinking

The capacity of information systems to function in a logical, sequential and rational fashion. Equated to "particle" thinking because the process resembles the behavior of particles.

Macroscopic

Large enough to be seen by the naked eye, for scales down to 0.01 mm. Scales below this are referred to as microscopic.

Maxwell field

The synthesis of electricity, magnetism and light into dynamic fields that can oscillate and move through space.

Mechanisms of consciousness

The biophysical mechanisms directly associated with the function of consciousness.

Menu of options

The sum of all possibilities of any set of circumstances.

Microtubules

Small tubes (approximately 23 nanometers in diameter) that form the cytoskeleton of the cells and contain the capacity to store and disseminate information. Thought to be a key mechanism to consciousness, mitosis, cell growth, organ growth and quantum coherence in the body.

Multidimensional

An information field composed of more than one unique measurable coordinate. This universe is composed of multidimensional information fields. Consciousness is also multidimensional.

M-theory
Attempts to unite all five string theories, as well as supergravity, within a single theoretical framework, but which is not yet fully understood.

Newton's Laws of Motion
Laws describing the motion of bodies based on the conception of absolute space and time. These held sway until Einstein's discovery of special relativity.

No boundary conditions
The idea that the universe is finite but has no boundary in imaginary time.

Parallel worlds
Universes running in parallel to ours and evidenced through their supergravitational fields and their impact upon this field of consciousness.

P-brane
A brane with *p* dimensions where *p* is a number. Also refer to *brane*.

Particle
Describes a standing wave or spinner that exists only at one point in time.

Potential
Refers to a possible manifestation in a given set of circumstances.

Pre-computed
Computations made that may have influence prior to conscious realization. Used in context of hyperspacial computations within one dimension (beyond time) that affect another (within time).

Presence
The ability of information systems to function on higher p-brane dimensions that include the influences of the hyperspacial counterpart or Full Potential Self of individuals or collectives.

Quantum
An indivisible unit of wave dynamics.

Quantum potential fields
The matrixes of information that exist through space and time. Such fields constitute one of the theoretical foundations of quantum physics and are thought to make up the majority of reality.

Quantum mechanics
The physical laws that govern the realm of the very small, such as atoms and protons.

Quantum frequencies

The measure of very small waves in terms of the number of complete cycles per second as are characteristic of consciousness and found within the microtubules of the body.

Space-time

This four-dimensional space whose points are events.

Spatial dimension

Any of the space-time dimensions (as in depth, width, height and time) that constituted physical experience.

Special Relativity

Einstein's theory based upon the idea that the laws of science should be the same for all observers, no matter how they are moving, in the absence of gravitational fields.

Spin

An internal property of elementary particles, related to but not identical to the everyday notion of spin, but related to the properties of information transmitted from hyperspace.

Stages of development

From developmental psychology, the stages of development refer to specific stages each person goes through in life: conception, in vitro, birth, early childhood, young adult, marriage, career, family, midlife, golden years, declining years and death. Consciousness emerges during these stages according to its own implicate patterns.

String

A fundamental, one-dimensional object in string theory that replaces the concept of structureless elementary particles. Different vibration patterns of a string give rise to elementary particles with different properties. Similar functions are evident within information fields of consciousness that give rise to different belief systems among humans.

String theory

Also known as superstring theory that explains particles as waves on strings and attempts to unite quantum mechanics and general relativity.

Superconductivity

Superconductivity is the ability of certain materials to conduct electrical current with low resistance and extremely low losses and is now possible at high temperatures via infused ceramic superconductors.

Supergravity

A set of theories unifying general relativity and supersymmetry.

Supersymmetry

A principle that relates the properties of particles of different spin. Consciousness is thought to operate on supersymmetry principles.

Swarm intelligence

The ability of some species, such as ants, termites, fish, birds and humans, to act as one collectively conscious entity. This ability is thought to be a function of the quantum dynamics within microtubules that function hyperspacially.

Telepathic tunneling

The ability of microtubules (or other life forms) to share information without any visible means of transferring this information. Thought to be a demonstration of quantum frequencies (Frohlech) that transmit information via hyperspacial wormholes directly from within the microtubules.

Thermodynamics

The study of the relationship between energy, work, heat, and entropy in a dynamic physical system.

Time dilation

A feature of special relativity predicting that the flow of time will slow for an observer in motion or in the presence of a strong gravitational field.

Time loop

Another name for a closed, time-like curve. Similar to aspects of conscious experiences reflecting time dilations.

Topology

The schematic representation of the mathematics of abstract concepts as in the topology of the "mind model" showing a schematic drawing of the various dimensions involved in consciousness.

Transform

To change in form. Information systems cannot, according to the laws of conservation, be created or destroyed. They can only be changed in form.

Uncertainty principle

The principle formulated by Heisenberg that one can never be exactly sure of both the position and the velocity of a particle. The more accurately one know the one, the less accurately one knows the other. One cannot weigh a running horse.

Unified Theory

Any theory that describes all four forces and all of matter within a single framework.

Vacuum energy

Energy that is present in apparent empty space. Thought to cause the expansion of the universe to speed up.

Virtual particle

A particle that can never be directly detected but whose existence has measurable effects.

Vortex energies

The forces associated with spinning wave dynamics.

Wave dynamics

Also known as wave function, wave dynamics are a fundamental concept of quantum mechanics and declare that a number at each point in space associated with a particle; determines the probability that the particle is to be found at that position.

Wave/particle duality

The concept that there are no distinctions between particles and waves. Particles are considered to be like waves, and visa versa.

Wormhole

A thin tube of space-time connecting distant regions of the universe. Wormholes may link parallel universes and could provide the possibility of time travel. They also may be a function of mental health.

ACKNOWLEDGEMENTS

A very special thanks to Stephen Hawking, David Bohm, Michael Talbot, Ken Wilber and others, who may not be referenced herein, for laying the foundation for this *Therapy Manifesto and the 95 Treatises on Holodynamic Therapy*. The value of your work cannot be measured but it is, nevertheless, appreciated and has helped to create extraordinary results in the world of therapy.

My gratitude is also extended to the first "real" therapist to impact my life. In 1971, when I was enrolled in my doctorate program in developmental psychology at Brigham Young University, Phil McQueen, from Antioch University, taught one of my first doctorial classes. His mastery of therapy helped me unveil the enfolded dimensions of my own consciousness. His was the powerful touch of a holodynamic mind. My thanks to Phil cannot be overstated.

I also acknowledge the help of Sandy Pendleton, my friend and colleague, who is a holodynamic therapist and who helped support me through this writing.

Some of you may be aware that around the world there are individuals and groups of people who have discovered the Holodynamics of reality and, each in their own way, are applying themselves to unfolding life potential. I would like to recognize a few.

As special recognition is extended to Luba Hocklova, in Moscow, Russia, and her team of more than 100 psychologists who have been using Holodynamic Therapy in Russia and the CIS Republics. Your countries have undergone cataclysmic changes in the past two decades but few are aware of the superhuman efforts that people like you and your colleagues have extended in helping people learn to live in a world that has changed so much in such little time. Congratulations to each of you!

There is another group of people in the Middle East who have been working to potentialize a sustainable community. Known as "The Order of the River of Life," their goal is to help people who have been involved in conflicts, to shift their consciousness to a life beyond war. May you "work your way out of a job" as soon as possible. Until then, the holodynamic world cheers you on.

Also, among the Israeli community there are certain people who have discovered the Holodynamic reality and are dedicated to aiding even the extremes of fundamentalism to unfold their fullest potential. You are pioneering a new horizon on the unclaimed territories of human consciousness. My congratulations I send to each and every one of you.

I send my appreciation and my support to all holodynamists who are creating such extraordinary results in shifting the consciousness of humanity and creating a more sustainable future – one that is mentally healthy.

REFERENCES

Beksey Von, G. *Sensory Inhibition,* Princeton University Press, Princeton

Blue, R & Blue, W. *Correlational Opponent Processing: A Unifying Principle* (1996) Available at http://www.enticypress.com

Bohm, David. *Wholeness and the Implicate Order,* London, Routledge & Kagen, 1980

Bohm, David and F. David Peat. *Science, Order, and Creativity,* New York: Bantam Books, 1987

Bracewell, R. N. *The Fourier Transform and its Application,* McGraw-Hill, New York

Brown, W. *Laws of Form,* 1964

Carse, James C. *Finite and Infinite Games,* 1994

Chalmers, D. *The Puzzle of Conscious Experience, Scientific American,* Dec. 1995

Chew, G. S. *The Analytic S-Matrix. A Basis for Nuclear Democracy,* Benjamin, New York

Daugman, F. G. "Uncertainty Relation for Resolution in Space, Spatial Frequency, and Orientation Optimized by Two Dimensional Visual Cortical Filters," *Journal of the Optical Society of America,* 2(7), pp. 1160-1169, 1985

Freeman, W. "Correlation of Electrical Activity of Prepyriform Cortex and Behavior in a Cat," *Journal of Neurophysiology,* 23, pp. 111-131.

Frohlech, H. "Long-range Coherence and Energy Storage in Biological Systems," *Journal of Quantum Chemistry,* II, pp. 641-649, 1968

Gabor, D. "Theory of Communication," *Institute of Electrical Engineers,* 93, pp. 429-441, 1946

Ghahramani, Z. & Wolpert, D. "Modular Decomposition in Visumotor Learning," *Nature* pg. 392-395. (1997, March 27).

Gorgiev, Danco Dimchev. "Impairment of consciousness in Alzheimer's disease: the amyloid water-filled nanotubes manifest quantum optical coherence interfering with the normal quantum brain dynamics?" *Journal of Psychiatry and Neurology,* 2002, available at www.dreamwater.org

Hameroff, S. R. *Information in Processing in Microtubules,* Journal of Theoretical Biology, pp. 98 549-61, 1982

Hameroff, S. R. and Penrose, Roger. *Conscious Events as Orchestrated Space-time Selections,* Journal of Consciousness Studies, 3, No. 1, 1996 p. 36-53

Hawking, Stephen. *The Universe in a Nutshell,* Bantam Books (2001)

Heisenberg, W. *Physics and Philosophy,* Allan and Unwin, 1959

Hempfling, Lee Kent. *The Neutronics Dynamic System,* Enticy Press (1994, 1996)

Hempfling, Lee Kent. *The Rotating Turtle,* Enticy Press (1998).

Kane, B. E. "A Silicon-Based Nuclear Spin Quantum Computer," *Nature,* vol. 393 pg.133 (1998, May 14)

Kant, I. in **Wilber, Ken.** *The Eye of Spirit, An Integral Vision for a World Gone Slightly Mad,* Shambhala, Boston and London, 1997

Kelly, Kevin. *Out of Control: The New Biology Machines, Economic Systems and the Social World,* 1995

Kohlberg, Lawrence. "Essays on Moral Development," Vol. I, *The Philosophy of Moral Development,* San Francisco, Harper and Row, 1981

Levine, Rick et al. *The Cluetrain Manifesto: the End of Business as Usual,* 2001

Luoma, Jon R. *The hidden forest: The Biography of an Ecosystem,* 1999.

Marcelja, S. "Mathematical Description of the Response of Simple Cortical Cells," *Journal of the Optical Society of America,* 70, pp. 1297-1300, 1980.

MacKay, David J.C. *Information Theory, Pattern Recognition and Neural Networks,* Cambridge University Press, 2005

Murchie, Guy. *Seven Mysteries of Life: an Exploration in Science and Philosophy,* Houton Miphlan, 1978

Pearce, Joseph C. *Evolution's End,* Harper Collins, 1993

Penrose, Roger. *Shadows of the Mind,* Oxford University Press 1994

Piaget, J. *The Child's Conception of the World,* New York, Humanities 1951

Plato, in **Wilber, Ken.** *The Eye of Spirit, An Integral Vision for a World Gone Slightly Mad,* Boston and London, Shambhala, 1997

Pribram, Karl. *Brain and Perception: Holonomy and Structure in Figural Processing,* Lawrence Erlbaum Assoc., New Jersey 1991

Pribram, Karl. "Quantum Information Processing and the Spiritual Nature of Mankind," *Frontier Perspectives, 6,* (1), pp. 12-15, 1996

Prigogene, Ilya. *Order Out of Chaos,* Bantam New Age, 1984

Rector, K., and Woolf, Victor Vernon. *The Ten Processes of Holodynamics,* 1964, available at http://www.holodynamics.com/store

Rector, K. *Holodynamic Tracking,* 1997 available at http://www.holodynamics.com

RICCI the Robot, available at http://www.neutronicstechcorp.com/private

Sheldrake, Rupert. *A New Science of Life,* 1981

Sheldrake, Rupert. *Chaos, Creativity and Cosmic Consciousness,* 2001

Spencer, Ronald G. *Exploring the Use of PNP Bipolar and MOSFET Transistors in Implementing the Neutronics Dynamic System,* Enticy Press (1997)

Schauberger, Viktor. *The Energy Evolution,* edited by Callum Coats, 2000

Scott, A. *Stairway to the Mind,* Copernicus, New York, 1995

Talbot, Mike. *The Holographic Universe,* 1992

Thomas, Lewis. *Lives of a Cell: Notes of a Biology Watcher,* Bantam Books, 1974

Umbanhowar, Paul B. Melo, Francisco and Swinney, Harry L. "Localized excitations in a vertically vibrated granular layer." *Nature, pp.* 793-796. (1996, August)

Vannucci, M. and Corradi. F (1997, May). *Some findings on the covariance structure of wavelet coefficients: Theory and models in a Bayesian perspective.* unpublished report UKC/IMLS/97/05

Wheeler, J. A. "Assessment of Everett's "relative state" formulation of quantum theory," Rev. Mod. Phys. 29, pp. 463-5, 1957

Wilber, Ken. *The Eye of Spirit, An Integral Vision for a World Gone Slightly Mad,* Boston and London, Shambhala, 1997

Wilber, Ken. *The Holographic Paradigm and Other Paradoxes,* 1982

Whitehead, A. N. *Process and Reality,* Macmillan, New York,1933

Wolf, Fred Alan. *Parallel Universes: The Search for Other Worlds,* Simon & Schuster, 1990.

Woolf, Victor Vernon. *Holodynamics: How to Manage Your Personal Power,* Harbinger House, 1990.

Woolf, Victor Vernon. *The Dance of Life: Transform your world NOW!* The International Academy of Holodynamics, 2005.

Woolf, Victor Vernon. *The Holodynamic State of Being: the Advocate's Manual I.* The International Academy of Holodynamics, 2005.

Woolf, Victor Vernon. *Presence in a Conscious Universe: the Consultant's Manual II.* The International Academy of Holodynamics, 2005.

Woolf, Victor Vernon. *Field Shifting: the Holodynamics of Integration.* The International Academy of Holodynamics, 2006.

Woolf, Victor Vernon. *Leadership and Team Building: the Holodynamics of Building a New World.* The International Academy of Holodynamics, 2006.

Woolf, Victor Vernon. *Principle-driven Transformation: the Holodynamics of the Dance of Life.* The International Academy of Holodynamics, 2006.

Woolf, Victor Vernon. *The Wellness Manifesto; 95 Treatises on Holodynamic Wellness.* The International Academy of Holodynamics, 2006.

Woolf, Victor Vernon. *ELVES: the Adventures of Nicholas: the Grid of Agony and the Field of Love.* The International Academy of Holodynamics, 2006.

Please note that all writings by Victor Vernon Woolf, Ph.D., can be purchased directly at www.holodynamics.com or at Ingram Books, Amazon.com or at your local book store.

Personal Footnote for those who desire to be more effective in dealing with people:

Most people are determined to move beyond such generalities as "helping others to find mental health." This treatise seeks to bring the entire field of therapy into a more scientifically grounded field of study. For me, the easiest way to demonstrate any aspect of service is to take a scientific view, study carefully what is being suggested, and then try it out myself. I ask myself what works and what does not work. Then, if it is theoretically consistent and it works, I teach it to others. Does it work for them in a similar manner as it worked for me? If not, why not? What can be done about it? Let's do it. Let's find what works and seek as good an explanation as possible.

For example, imagine a Place of Peace (take a minute). Now imagine in your Place of Peace, your Full Potential Self coming toward you. What kind of "being" are you? Of course you might want to study Roger Penrose's Orch (OR) theory and figure out the mathematical premises that show "networks of entangled spinner information systems pre-computed the collapse of the quantum field" in order to gain a more scientific knowledge about the possible relationship between the OR and the Full Potential Self.

Or, you may want to review Steven Hawking's summaries on "hyperspacial counterpart." You might want to work with the University of Arizona with Stewart Hameroff's consciousness studies and find out more about the microtubules. Or you may want to go onto the Internet and look up Gorgiev, in Budapest, and learn about "psychic tunneling."

Quantum physics, information theory, mathematics, vortex sciences and others take us closer to understanding consciousness. Kevin Kelly wrote a great book titled *Out of Control* that contains some good information about swarm intelligence.

The References contained herein have been helpful to me in my own exploration and so I refer you to them.

It is my conviction that the greater our understanding of reality, the greater our potential for understanding consciousness and the greater our effectiveness in life. The same is true of therapy.

Of course, the greatest breakthrough for me was when I moved beyond everything I had been taught or read in books. It occurred when I discovered my own Full Potential Self. My hyperspacial counterpart became my doorway into the enfolded dimensions of reality. It is within these enfolded dimensions that I found the solutions to my own problems and discovered the keys to helping others find their solutions, both personally and collectively. I am now convinced that everyone can become emotionally and mentally healthy. Outlined in this manifesto are some of the keys to unfolding this potential.

This manifesto is an open door. If you have comments or suggestions for further study, please let us know. Contact us at http://www. holodynamics.com

Printed in the United States
100909LV00007B/6/A

9 780974 643168